JEWS
AND
CHRISTIANS

◆

JEWS

—— AND ——

CHRISTIANS

◆

The Contemporary Meeting

A. Roy Eckardt

◆

Indiana University Press • *Bloomington*

Manufactured in the United States of America

Library of Congress Cataloging-in-Publication Data

Eckardt, A. Roy (Arthur Roy), 1918–
    Jews and Christians, the contemporary meeting.

    Bibliography: p.
    Includes index.
    1. Judaism—Relations—Christianity—1945–
2. Christianity and other religions—Judaism—1945–
I. Title.
BM535.E3   1986   261.2'6   85–45327
ISBN 0–253–33162–5

1 2 3 4 5 90 89 88 87 86

In memory of
URI TAL
My friend

Scholar of scholars

He knew the anguish,
He bore it bravely,
He kept the faith.

No one outside Israel can understand the mystery of Israel. And no one outside Christendom can understand the mystery of Christendom. . . . How is it possible for these mysteries to exist side by side? That is God's mystery.

—Martin Buber,
DIE STUNDE UND DIE ERKENNTNIS

CONTENTS

PREFACE

I endeavor here to depict and to assess the contemporary encounter of Jews and Christians. Readers will quickly be struck by the book's omissions, sketchiness, and debatable generalizations. I could try to excuse this state of affairs by protesting that the instructions from my publisher were to keep things brief. Instead, I marshall positive thinking, expressing the hope that the shortness and simplifications of the volume may actually enable the major thrusts (and parries) of today's Jewish-Christian meeting to break through. Yet a more formidable complication remains: my penchant is largely toward intellectuality; this raises the specter of elitism.

Part I, "Foundations," and Part II, "Lineaments of Today's Meeting," seek to sketch and to reckon with the structure and the stuff of the Jewish-Christian vis-à-vis. Part III, "Where the Action Is," attends to a few practical areas of current controversy and collaboration. Part IV, "Searchable Judgments," is an elliptic venture in valuation. Yet none of the categories—descriptive exposition, moral praxis, and critical apprais-al—is entirely absent from the whole.

The materials I introduce point to a number of genres: social, psycho-logical, moral, theological, and religious. I tend to feel that social data are best handled sociologically, moral issues ethically, religious data re-ligiously, etc. This is a debatable stance. When in a few places I resort to a religious way of speaking, the "language of ultimate concern" (Terence Des Pres, following Paul Tillich), this does not perforce mean that the reader is being "preached" at. The problem for a scholar is how to be faithful to the data and ideas that are competing for delineation—how, so to speak, to treat them from within. Granting a due place for critical and personal response, I believe that an adequate phenomenology will try to project itself into the points of view being presented. There are limits here; we are hardly to identify, for example, with the viewpoint of Nazi criminals. Such a methodology does not guarantee that arbitrariness and bias will be forestalled. Yet I agree with Professor Des Pres in *The Survivor* that to "write about terrible things in a neutral tone" is to end in "either cynicism or despair." Along this same line, I should not wish my methodological assumptions to turn into an apology for a certain form of religious faith—any more than I should wish them to become a subtle way of undermining faith. The point I am driving toward is that when, as in the present study, various kinds of data and ideas are synthesized, assigned meaning, and evaluated the overall effort may properly be construed as philosophic, or, more precisely, as a contribution to moral philosophy. This point coheres with Emil L. Fackenheim's conviction in his magisterial work *To Mend the World* "that one cannot be a modern Jewish thinker without also being a philosophical one." I am persuaded that this truth applies as well to a modern Christian thinker. But Professor Fackenheim adds, wisely, that "one cannot be both a Jewish and a Christian thinker."

I want this volume to point the way to the human significance of our subject but also to its intellectual-spiritual-moral vitality. And I trust that for all the obligation to inform and analyze, I do not disserve the duties of ethical decision-making and commitment. For whatever it is that divides Jews and Christians, they are yet bound timelessly within a vocation of moral judgment and moral responsibility.

I am as uncomfortable as anyone when writers parade their credentials before readers. Yet perhaps an understanding of this book and its purposes, and perhaps even of elements in the recent history of the Jewish-Christian meeting in this country, will be served a little by my noting a close personal involvement with our subject ever since 1944, a commitment that led to my first book, *Christianity and the Children of Israel* (1948). Some passages in chapters five and nine are adapted from an article by me in *Holocaust and Genocide Studies* (Oxford).

JEWS
AND
CHRISTIANS
◆

PART I

◆

Foundations

1

♦

Two Identities

I should hope that in a primal sense the book before the reader will be received as a children's story, i.e., a story for the sake of the children. The ground of this hope will be made evident.

A fundamental assumption of my work is that it is wrong to use a Christian point of view to argue to the insufficiency or invalidity of Jewish existence, and equally wrong to use a Jewish point of view to argue to the insufficiency or invalidity of Christian existence. I have maintained this presupposition over many years. However, such a posture does nothing in itself to overcome perplexing problems of approach and methodology.

As the subtitle of this volume intimates, I am going to stress recent and current trends (thinking and practice) in the relation of Jews and Christians. Historical data and background will be scant. For purposes of manageability yet with some reluctance I shall concentrate, though not exclusively, upon a contemporary American context and outlook. North America is one of the two major locales—the other is Israel—for today's Jewish-Christian encounter. However, a restriction to the American scene cannot but have a certain constraining effect.

I

How is a single individual to write intelligibly or constructively about the contemporary meeting of Jews and Christians? And what is to be the overall vantage point? To proceed only from the Jewish side would fail to represent Christians. But to speak exclusively from the Christian side would leave the Jewish voice unheard. Scholars are taught the virtue of impartiality. Among the difficulties in neutralism is that it has a way of taking a holiday from real-life identities, commitments, and controversies. And it tends to ignore the demand upon human beings to make responsible moral choices amidst daily assaults from evil and daily outpourings of good.

Is the above paragraph implying that such a project as the present one is unrealizable? If so, the more the pages pile up, the more will confusion reign. Yet what if, in contrast, something within the gathering language manages to hint at the feasibility of the project, at least fragmentarily so? Here comes the traditional author protestation of self-legitimacy, cloaking all the self-doubt. But without some such legitimation, where is the quittance in writing anything? It happens to be so that people are capable of entering into worlds beyond their own parochial world—though only when they are somehow granted essential aid from common grace: understanding, empathy, and experience. And in the present case, steps toward such transcendence can be ventured because the Jewish world and the Christian world are not incommensurate. In the epigraph to this volume Martin Buber is contending that the mystery of Israel and the mystery of Christendom may only be grasped from within. But does the Christian stand wholly outside Israel? And does the Jew stand wholly outside Christendom?

Whether it is licit to assemble generalizations, even cautious ones, respecting Jewish identity and a Jewish point of view, or respecting Christian identity and a Christian point of view, is a moot and nagging question. I shall try to be as representative and fair as I can, keeping in mind that a minority persuasion or interpretation and a majority or ruling one are different things. At the same time I am sure that my depictions of what is "representative" (whether Jewish or Christian) will be subjected to keen judgment and refinement by critics.

II

The reality of Jewish identity and the reality of Christian identity are at once affinal and discontinuous. In both instances historical (history-stressing) faiths are involved, the faith known as Judaism and the faith known as Christianity. The Christian faith derives very largely from Judaism. But there is a telling discontinuity: It is by virtue of birth that a Jew *is* a Jew, while it is by virtue of some kind of decision or confession that a Christian *becomes* a Christian. Accordingly, to be a Jew a human being does not have to be a believing religionist. There is the integral identity of Jewish laic reality (*laos*, people), a non-racial reality and even a trans-ethnic reality. The truth that Jewish identity transcends both ethnic reality in the usual sense and also racial identification is brought home forcefully by the plurality-in-unity of the Jews of Israel, coming as they do from scores of countries with a great variety of ethnic backgrounds and racial differences. We think, for example, of the recently rescued community of Ethiopian Jews in Israel. In a phrase from the British historian James Parkes, Jewish identity is manifest in a "natural community" (an understanding not meant to contradict a confessed origin in the will of God). This helps explain how law *(halakhah)* has always been so fundamental to Judaism and the Jewish outlook: there is a primary and continuing need to administer and bless everyday, worldly life.

By contrast, to be a Christian is to become a believer in certain affirmations propounded by the Christian religion. In Christianness—a word here invented as a needed analytical counterpart to Jewishness—faith is the *sine qua non*. Jewishness is the matrix of Judaism, but that kind of relation does not apply between Christianness and Christian faith. When or if Jews abandon their faith they do not cease being Jews. They may no longer be "good" Jews from the standpoint of Jewish religionists, but they are still Jews. With Christians, a loss of faith entails, in principle, a loss of positive Christian identity.

I speak now in general terms. Even within the Christian community the act of participating in Christian peopleness in a cultural sense, and sometimes a national one, has upon occasion overridden the stipulation of an active or distinctive faith. Nor are we permitted to overlook socio-economic influences within a post-industrial America, e.g., the effects of middle-class interests upon the outlook of Protestants and Catholics (as also of Jews). Again, some Jews, including respected authorities, continue to deem the praxis of faith, i.e., religious belief-action, as a necessity for there to be authentic Jewishness. The strength of the link between Jewishness and the Jewish faith is manifest in the majority Jewish holding that any Jew who embraces Christianity or some other religion has to all intents and purposes opted out of the Jewish community.[1] In the same way, a convert to Judaism is deemed fully a Jew.

With due allowance for the above complications on both sides, one scholar's comparative description reflects the prevailing state of affairs: "In contrast to the Christian, for whom the rejection of a religious paradigm entails separation from the Christian community, many Jews find it possible to define and legitimate their continued Jewish identity in secular terms. Thus, while the notion of a secular Christian, who, rejecting any and all theological presuppositions, still professes Christianity, is inherently paradoxical, the notion of a secular Jew is not."[2]

To be sure, American Christians may present special ethnic features: Polish, African, Swedish, Hispanic, etc. Americans come in all shapes, colors, and sizes. But this is not of determining consequence for our particular subject. For American Jews as well can be identified within the above wider context: as people of Russian, German, Spanish, etc. background. In our comparative frame of reference the decisive fact is that the ethnic identities of American Christians are not independently intrinsic to or definitive for their *Christian* identity, whereas the laic identity of Jews is surely integral to their Jewishness.

If Jewish identity is constituted of Jewish peopleness (often with, yet sometimes without, the affirmations of a religious faith) while essential Christian identity definitely presupposes a particular faith, the consequences for practical Jewish-Christian relations are enormous. For the overall relation is then not describable as only a meeting between two different religions. But neither does the relation consist simply in an encounter of two different peoples. The religious dimension of the meeting is unavoidable.

There is the additional salient fact that in the United States, Jews and Christians meet as members and claimants of a common, distinctive culture that transcends Jewishness and Christianness. They participate in the ethos and resources of American society. They are Americans—with all the rights, privileges, immunities, honors, hazards, limitations, and sins thereunto appertaining. Needless to say, nothing in this shared state of affairs guarantees harmony or promises reconciliation. American culture is heterogeneous (as are the Jewish and Christian communities themselves) and that culture is anything but free of conflictive moral and political norms and behavior. Nor are the society's norms and behavior always consistent with Jewish and Christian norms. Thus are we met with the enlivening truth that in the public domain and marketplace Jews will sometimes range themselves with Christians against other Jews, while Christians will sometimes range themselves with Jews against other Christians. (This state of affairs will be exemplified in Part III.)

However, the shared participation in American culture is hardly that of numerical or social equals. Jews comprise a small and probably decreasing minority, fewer than three percent of the country's population. (The contribution of the Jewish community to American culture is disproportionate to its size.) Christians remain the prevailing majority in the United States. Indeed, at present there is a burgeoning Christian shift to the religious and political right, a move that can have grave consequences for interfaith and intergroup amity. In the United States the power of the people still means very largely the power of Christians and gentiles. It is a truism of moral and social philosophy that total evenhandedness in policy and action does not always end up like that but has a way of favoring majority possessors of power. Does this not pose a moral challenge to provide special representation and advocacy for minorities, if justice is going to be done?

I sometimes wonder about the feelings of Jews when they are assailed by radio and television summonses to repent and be saved by Jesus Christ. The Christian, even the most nominal or secularized one, experiences little of the trauma that such summonses potentially bring to the Jew. For to Jews the summonses constitute much more than a merely religious call. (Repentance is, after all, a staple of Judaism.) Such summonses are a stern reminder of the uncertainties and threats that are constitutive of minority status.

The Jewish condition in America is yet, ideally speaking, one of free human beings (in the traditional American understanding of freedom of thought, speech, opportunity, etc.)—this in marked contrast to Jewish historical experience in Europe, Asia, and Africa. For all the continuing menace of antisemitism,* Jewish life in the United States and Canada differs favorably from all other traditional fortunes of this people. Accordingly, any true comprehension of Jewish identity in America has to be "as much concerned with what America was and is still becoming as it is with the inner dynamics of Jewish life."[3] *Mutatis mutandis*, a comparable observation is to be made concerning Christian identity in America. And yet once all this is said, the American Jewish community, in contradistinction to the Jews of Israel, still lives within a largely extra-Jewish culture, a condition not paralleled amongst the vast multitude of American Christians.

---

*The late James Parkes used to refer to the spelling "anti-Semitism" as "pseudo-scientific mumbo jumbo." There is no such thing as a campaign against "Semitism." Since "antisemitism" is not a scientific word, it deserves neither a capital nor a hyphen. "Antisemitism" is possessed of a single and singular meaning: enmity to Jews as Jews (*Judenfeindschaft*).

III

What, then, is the special rationale for concentrating upon relations between Jews and Christians?

There is the inescapable truth that historically and substantively, Judaism and Christianity have never quite severed their parent-child relationship. The identity and problems of a child are closely tied to the reality and authority of parents—much more so than the converse. And the consequent brittleness and anguish never wholly disappear. The Christian community as a whole retains peculiar and powerful love-hate dispositions vis-à-vis the Jewish community and individual Jews. The destructiveness of Christian antisemitism and anti-Judaism persists.

The ongoing majority-minority relation of American Christians and Jews is thus complicated by an asymmetry created by centuries of historical influence and hostile Christian theological teaching. This makes misleading any treatment of the purpose and meaning of "the Jewish-Christian dialogue" as a matter only of mutual understanding and acceptance. Jews and Christians surely come to that dialogue in their claims as equal human beings, and they alike seek acceptance from the other. But they are not equal with respect to the weight of history, the weight of special sin. The Jew cannot overcome all suspiciousness. And the Christian cannot help but be disconcerted by flashbacks to the unhappy Christian past. On the whole, Jews as Jews have done nothing to hurt Christians; instead, they have helped them immeasurably. This can scarcely be said of Christians as Christians. The anti-Judaism and the anti-Jewishness of Christians and the Christian church find no comparable place in anti-Christianness among Jews. (Such Jewish anti-Christianness as there is is primarily a reaction to Christian anti-Judaism and antisemitism.) The Christian side carries moral scars and moral afflictions that are not found on the Jewish side.

It follows that the Jewish-Christian dialogue and relationship will exhibit both sameness of motivation and difference of motivation. For Jews, among the major questions are: What can we, as Jews and as Americans, contribute to human understanding and wellbeing, including the wellbeing of the Christian community and of our country? But also, what are we obliged to do to secure and maintain our own rightful interests and integrity along with other religious and ethnic minorities? For Christians, among the major questions are: What can we, as Christians and as

Americans, contribute to human understanding and wellbeing, including the wellbeing of the Jewish community and of our country? But also, what are we required to do to atone for and to overcome our woeful Christian heritage of antisemitism and anti-Judaism?

To bring together the exposition thus far: The identity of Jews in America involves three basic elements: peopleness (a *laos*); a faith within that peopleness, yet a faith that is not an absolute condition of Jewishness; and Americanness. The identity of Christians in this country involves two basic elements: a particular faith; and Americanness. The huge complexities within these five variables underlie the dialectic and the subject matter, and hence the impossible possibility, of this book. A question that does not go away for Jews is, How decisive is Judaism to Jewishness? In contrast, and with full awareness of the thousands of very nominal Christians, any question of how decisive Christian faith is to Christianness is not very meaningful. Finally, the relation of Jews and Christians points to the burden of a long history. All in all, the contemporary Jewish-Christian meeting—factually, morally, and theologically construed—is symmetrical and also asymmetrical.

2

♦

The Inveterate Vis-à-Vis

Donald A. Hagner contends that "to try to ignore or explain away the differences that separate Jews and Christians does not promote dialogue; it obstructs it."[1] As suggested in chapter one, such a judgment rightfully applies to discrepancies of historical experience and moral behavior. But it applies as well to differences of religious and existential affirmation and commitment. Hagner is speaking of the latter genre of differences.

I

Jews and Christians share a trust in and celebration of the reality and authority of the one God. It is ironic, therefore, that the Jewish-Christian vis-à-vis first arose out of a strictly religious conflict. The conflict, occasioned by the advent of Christianity, is made to persist by virtue of Christianity's enduringness. True, in most recent years the meeting of Jews and Christians has been transforming itself, from the Christian side as well as from the Jewish side. Later pages will ring these developments. Nevertheless, the changes and new ventures have by no means dissolved the stuff of nineteen centuries. This chapter concentrates upon the traditional encounter and conflict in its historically dominant yet still assertive forms and expressions.

Judaism and the community of Israel long antedate the church. It is often pointed out that Jews as Jews have no particular need to concern themselves with Christianity, since Christianity poses no special or commanding questions for the Jewish community. The Jewish-Christian controversy, past and present, derives from the Christian claim. Rightfully or wrongfully, traditional Christianity sees itself as the fulfillment of Judaism. This means that something within Christianity always stands in judgment upon Judaism and Jewishness—or strives to do so. Overall, the dominating character of the historic Christian community's attitude to Judaism and the Jewish people has been one of *ambivalence:* a full acceptance and recognition of Israel as the *fons et origo* of the Christian faith, and concerted judgments against Israel for (reputedly) denying its own consummation in the Lord Jesus Christ. The church rests upon the foundation of Israel, but it identifies itself as the new Israel, the true Israel.

The most exclusivist or anti-Jewish advocate of Christianity can scarcely ignore the truth that the Christian edifice is reared out of Jewishness and Judaism. It would be hard to excise Abraham, Isaac, Moses, Isaiah, and Jeremiah from the church's collective memory and life. It would be difficult to blot out Exodus, Temple, Exile, and the coming of the synagogue. For that matter, it is not easy for the church to show its back to someone else who was a faithful Jew from beginning to end: Jesus of Nazareth. (Yet the Nazis and their "German Christian" collaborators conjured up these very tricks.)

Everything turns upon how Christians have responded and are to respond to the above and other Jewish realities. One determining outlook within the Christian community has been to treat Jewishness as though it involves no more than a religion (and a dubious and even false religion at that). Ironically, portents of such reductionism manifested themselves in the transworldly spiritualizing and de-Judaizing process that was soon to characterize the Christian corpus as the reputed continuation and successor of Judaism. The gentile church took Jewish expectations and prophetic hopes of a considerably world-oriented and even socio-political nature—expectations and hopes that of course presupposed the authority and governance of the Ruler of history—and transfigured them into a prevailing schema of individual sin–repentance–salvation, this in only limited consonance with inherited Jewish teachings. The object of Torah Judaism is the sanctification of all life *(haim),*[2] while Christianity has tended to make "the salvation of the soul" its raison d'être. For everything was changed through the work of the apostle Paul and others, who appropriated the small, strictly Jewish and Pharisee fellowship of Jesus and his followers[3] and created the new religion of Christianity. The historical, coming reign of God for which Jesus, a Torah-loving Jew, evidently gave his life, an effort that extended to a hoped-for restoration of the promised land to the people of God,[4] was soon radically altered into a kingship "not of this world" (John 18:36). True, the worldly divine reign kept seeking to establish itself, as in the holy empire of Christendom and the later Christian commonwealths of Calvinists and Puritans. But withal, religiousness has ever and again won the day within Christianity.

Insofar as Jewishness means peopleness, today's State of Israel need present no theological-moral embarrassment to Jews. But insofar as Christianity means religiousness, the secular-political corpus of Vatican City remains a small thorn in the Christian community's theological-moral side, as yet at the same time in the United States "the separation of church and state" persists as a commitment not just of unbelievers, but amongst unnumbered Christian devout. These examples, Jewish and Christian, reflect tellingly Jewish identity and Christian identity in their contemporary disparity. Yet here as elsewhere the matter is not quite so simple. No group in the United States opposes potential and overt alliances of church and state more than the Jewish community; here enters the variable of Jewish Americanness listed at the end of chapter one. For that matter, the State of Israel is hardly a theocracy, it has no state religion, and freedom of religion abounds there. (An ironic exception is restrictions, not upon non-Jews, but upon non-Orthodox Jews—for example, in the exclusive right of Orthodox rabbis to solemnize marriages.) To complete the picture, a readiness to breach the wall between religion and state is not absent from certain groups within today's American Christianity.

II

It is so that Jewish insistences upon the sanctity of life, the struggle against idolatry, and the requirement of justice have universalist and religious import. In principle, the obligations of righteousness are thereby directed to all humankind. In the Jewish tradition, non-Jews are seen as subject to the Noachian laws or covenant (named after Noah): the prohibitions against blasphemy, theft, idolatry, murder, incest, and the consumption of flesh taken from living animals, plus the obligation to maintain courts of justice. Thus is made possible the Jewish persuasion that "the righteous of the nations" have a share in the world-to-come (olam ha-ba). Furthermore, the love and care of God encompass non-Jews. The rabbi of Koznitz used to repeat the quixotic prayer, "If You do not yet wish to redeem Israel, at any rate redeem the goyim."[5]

The expectation has never been wholly lost that all humankind must eventually see the truth of the special kind of monotheism that Judaism proclaims. However, historically and practically this expectation has been downplayed and tends to be construed eschatologically. Decisively, such an expectation has not served as a ground of external social or religious policy on the part of Jews. Here is a sharp contrast with the traditional missionary thrust of Christianity. For the direction taken by day-to-day *Judaism* is quite another matter from general moral standards and eschatological hopes, if of course not a wholly separable one. That direction is inward. Judaism's discrete fealty to God and the Torah (Guidance) of God is, in the first instance, an internal business, i.e., a commitment within and for Israel, the Jewish community. This is how the religious claim of Judaism has always avoided imperialism and intolerance toward other faiths. At most, any evidently imperialist aspects of the Judaic claim are turned upon Jews themselves—specific individuals who perhaps have problems honoring that claim, or who fail to accept it, or who, being female, are remanded, in effect, to second-class citizenship within the community (see chap. 7).

By contrast, Christian demands have always been directed outward as much as inward. Their application to Jews (and others) derives from reputed spiritual truth of an absolute and universalist kind. In principle, while Judaism applies to Jews, Christianity is oriented to everybody and anybody. This is how any "Jewish mission to Christians" has had little substantive place, whereas "the Christian mission to Jews" has had historic meaning. (We shall be noting some interesting, partial changes here on both sides.)

On the one hand, then, the claim of the Christian church has been held to extend peculiarly to Jews *as Jews*, and, on the other hand, that claim, applying as it does to all humankind, has been held to extend to Jews *as human beings*. It is from out of these two powerful and interrelated facts that the Jewish-Christian conflict arises.

III

There are three treasures. The treasure of Jewishness is the integrity of Jewish life, with implications for the sanctity of all life. The treasure of Judaism is the Torah of God. The treasure of Christianity is Jesus Christ.

The third of these treasures constitutes the bone of contention. For that treasure is held to embody a crisis, especially for the second treasure yet even for the first.

The Christian claim for Jesus Christ centers in the threefold In-carnation-Crucifixion-Resurrection as this is documented in and inspired by the New Testament. Here are sample representations of the three elements:

(a) In the beginning was the Word, . . . and the Word was God. . . . all things were made through him. . . . In him was life, and the life was the light of men. . . . He came to his own home, and his own people [the Jews] received him not. But to all who received him, who believed in his name, he gave power to become children of God; who were born, not of blood nor of the will of the flesh nor of the will of man, but of God.

And the Word became flesh and dwelt among us, full of grace and truth; . . . For the law was given through Moses; grace and truth came through Jesus Christ (John 1:1, 3, 4, 11–14, 17).

(b) He [Pilate] said to the Jews, "Behold your King!" They cried out, "Away with him, away with him, crucify him!" Pilate said to them, "Shall I crucify your King?" The chief priests answered, "We have no king but Caesar." Then he handed him over to them to be crucified.

So they took Jesus . . . to the place called the place of a skull, . . . There they crucified him (John 19:14–18).

For the word of the cross is folly to those who are perishing, but to us who are being saved it is the power of God. . . . For Jews demand signs and Greeks seek wisdom, but we preach Christ crucified, a stumbling block to Jews and folly to Gentiles, but to those who are called, both Jews and Greeks, Christ the power of God and the wisdom of God (I Cor. 1:18, 22–24).

And he died for all, that those who live might live no longer for themselves but for him who for their sake died and was raised (II Cor. 5:15).

(c) He said to them, "Do not be amazed; you seek Jesus of Nazareth, who was crucified. He has risen, he is not here; see the place where they laid him" (Mark 16:6).

Jesus said to her, "I am the resurrection and the life; he who believes in me, though he die, yet shall he live, and whoever lives and believes in me shall never die" (John 11:25–26).

[God raised Christ] from the dead and made him sit at his right hand in the heavenly places (Eph. 1:20).

If Christ has not been raised, your faith is futile and you are still in your sins (I Cor. 15:17).

There is salvation in no one else, for there is no other name under heaven given among men by which we must be saved (Acts 4:12).

> God has highly exalted him and bestowed on him the name which is above every name, that at the name of Jesus every knee should bow . . . and every tongue confess that Jesus Christ is Lord, to the glory of God the Father (Phil. 2:9–11).

We note that these avowals are anything but merely personal-confessional in nature (such as, say, the wording in the act of marriage, where bride and groom only promise to honor and keep each other, disregarding anyone else). In essential contrast to this, the New Testament declarations are put forward as objectively valid, universal truths applicable, in principle, to every human being. Thus is it asserted to be a fact that Jesus Christ, the Word of God, is the light of men (not just some men); that he, unlike Moses, brought grace and truth; that he died for all; that to believe in the resurrected Christ is to be saved from death; and that there is salvation in no one but him. In sum: "I am the way, and the truth, and the life; no one comes to the Father, but by me" (John 14:6).

We note as well that the New Testament documents match the fealty of Christians to Jesus Christ with his (alleged) rejection by faithless Jews. "The Jews" (reputedly) spurned him and took reprehensible part in killing him. Indeed, the Gospel of John has Jesus identify "the Jews" as children of the devil (8:44). And it emphasizes that he who does not believe in Christ "is condemned already, because he has not believed in the name of the only Son of God" (3:18). To reject Christ is to open oneself to rejection by God.

This majority New Testament position of anti-Judaism and anti-Jewishness reaches a kind of climax in Romans 9–11. The Canadian Catholic scholar Gregory Baum goes so far as to maintain that efforts of Christian theologians to draw a different conclusion "are grounded in wishful thinking. What Paul and the entire Christian tradition taught is unmistakably negative: the religion of Israel is now superseded, . . . the promises fulfilled in the Christian church, the Jews struck with blindness, and whatever remains of the election to Israel rests as a burden upon them in the present age."[6] Paul's insistence that "God has not rejected his people" as the root of salvation (Rom. 11:2, 17–18) appears to temper somewhat the apostle's position but, on Baum's view—as well as that of E. P. Sanders and others—does not overcome it.

For nineteen hundred years the foregoing Christology and soteriology have been taught by the Christian church and continue to be taught and preached in great numbers of its branches and local congregations. Accordingly, to attend to the New Testament record does much more than return us to the ancient past. For these writings remain normative and authoritative for American and other Christians today. Decisively, Christians view the witness of the New Testament as pointing to the historical-divine consummation of the expectations of the so-called Old Testament (Hebrew Scripture, the *Tanak*) and hence as a fulfillment of, and judgment upon, Judaism and Jewishness.

This ongoing persuasion is exemplified contemporaneously by John Frederick Jansen of Austin Presbyterian Theological Seminary, with special reference to the Resurrection of Jesus Christ: "In the resurrection and vindication of Jesus the earliest church saw the completion and goal of Israel's faith in God." That faith "finds its ultimate expression" in the Easter faith of Christianity. "The whole of God's story with his people" is "fulfilled in the resurrection of Jesus. . . . All people do not yet accept Easter's pledge, but one day 'every eye will see him, every one who pierced him' (Rev. 1:7). . . . Ultimate vindication includes ultimate judgment. The risen Jesus 'is the one ordained by God to be judge of the living and the dead' (Acts 10:42)." The New Testament message "sees in Easter the surety of the future of Jesus Christ as Lord of all and Lord forever." The Easter faith reminds us that "the future of Jesus includes the future of Israel. . . . Israel's future is bound up with the future of Christ."[7]

Not atypically, Carroll E. Simcox of today's Foundation for Christian Theology sees in Jesus Christ the essential ground of any genuine relation with the neighbor. Citing Dietrich Bonhoeffer's contention that "we can only get in touch with our neighbors" through Christ, Simcox declares that

> Christ is the *only* mediator, here, there, everywhere, between God and human, and between human and human. As the eternal Logos of God he is God speaking, and we speak with, rather than to, each other only through him. He mediates not only divine reason, truth and meaning to us and among us, but all love: among all persons and indeed, among all living creatures. . . . Since that Word was made flesh and dwelt among us we know his name; and he is the same Word through whom all things are made, in whom all things consist, and by whom all communication is made possible.[8]

Something of the signs of the Christian times is shown in the fact that the mainline Protestant journal *The Christian Century*, known nationwide and internationally as a voice for Christian liberalism, should be publishing Simcox's piece together with other articles of like perspective.

The Christian emphasis of Simcox, in partial differentiation from that of Jansen, bears upon the church's attitude to all human beings, not just to Jews as Jews. There is a repeated note in the Christian tradition according to which it was the sin of all humankind that brought Jesus to the Cross. But—with some illogic—this has not meant the conclusion that the Buddhists of twentieth-century Japan are just as "guilty" as the Jews of first-century Judea. However, Carroll Simcox is clearly contending that any human communication even these Buddhists are able to attain with each other is made possible only by the hidden, unacknowledged spirit of Jesus Christ. And the same goes for all other people. Hence, contentions such as this have direct consequences for Christian attitudes to Jews together with reactive Jewish attitudes to the church.

In and through both emphases together, that of Jansen and that of Simcox, we are met by the two all-determinative facts listed at the end of section two of this chapter, and now with special reference to influential elements within contemporary American Christianity: the leveling of the Christian claim against Jews as Jews, and the leveling of the Christian claim against Jews as human beings.

IV

I have sketched the Christian claim in its dominant traditional form; in fairness, I shall do the same with the response of the Jewish community to Christianity.

The Jewish response has been threefold: (a) to ignore the Christian claim; (b) to characterize it as theologically untruthful and as contributive to immorality; and (c) to acknowledge, nevertheless, a certain legitimacy in Christianity and in Christian life. Let us develop these points.

(a) Through the centuries the Jewish community as a whole has never been impressed by the special religious claims of the church. (Here is found a most elementary explanation for why Jews have been uniquely singled out to receive the lashes of the church's antisemitism.)

It was mentioned above that nothing in Jewishness and Judaism as such requires any special preoccupation with Christianity. Jews have no internal religious or moral need for a vis-à-vis with the Christian community. The integrity of Jewishness is quite independent of Christianity. Accordingly, from a Jewish point of view the discrete Christian claims against Judaism and Jewishness can simply be disregarded. This applies to the person of Jesus, insofar as Jesus has been appropriated by the church. As Franz Rosenzweig once remarked, Christians "are usually very perplexed if one responds truthfully to their question: 'What does Judaism think about Jesus?' with the answer: 'Nothing.' "[9] The presumption of some Christian evangelists that Jews must decide whether they are going to say Yes or No to Jesus Christ is meaningless to Jews. They feel no such necessity. The presumption may say a lot about Christians; it says nothing about Jews. In contrast to all this—indeed implied by it—the Christians as Christians are the ones who have always been challenged by the presence of Judaism and Jewishness. They are required to say either Yes or No to Jews.

Christianity and Christians are not a problem for Jews; Judaism and Jews are a problem for Christians. However, the issue of the human need or lack of need of the one side for the other side is not quite so simple. For the sake of their survival, Jews cannot be oblivious to the moral desirability of Christian reformation. In this sense Jews do "need" Christians. On the other hand, Christians do not have to demand or expect anything from Jews for the sake of immediate Christian self-interest. In this respect Christians do not "need" Jews.

We are brought to a second consideration.

(b) Since in the real world of today's America encounters of Jews with Christians are in large measure unavoidable, Jews are obligated as Jewish human beings to answer attacks upon their integrity from Christian quarters. There is no way to do this responsibly apart from tacit and explicit moral and theological evaluation of the Christian claim and of the Christian judgments against Judaism.

On the Jewish view, Christianity is not the fulfillment of Judaism. That is to say, the Christological assertions made by the church are essentially false. By this is meant that God has no Son—though God does indeed have many sons and many daughters. The Messiah has not come. The world remains unredeemed. True, Jews evaluate differently one worldview and another. Thus, American democracy and German Nazism are at opposite moral poles. The minimal moral requirements of the Noachian laws are alluded to above. But the notion—much more widespread in Protestant than in Catholic Christianity—that you have to be "one of us" in order to be "saved" or to live rightly is, on a Jewish perspective, among the more unhappy forms of human pretension and immorality.

From the Jewish side, the treasures of the sanctity of life and of the Torah of God constitute a crisis for the church's treasure of Jesus as the Christ, rather than the other way round. The church is faced here by at least two problems: the authority of its New Testament, and the behavior of its people. On the one hand, the *Encyclopaedia Judaica* describes the New Testament as "the fountainhead of later Christian misrepresentation of Judaism and theological anti-Semitism."[10] On the other hand, were the claim that Jesus is the Christ in fact truthful, how could that claim have been followed by so many and such ceaseless Christian violations of the sanctity of Jewish life, by betrayals of the moral standards of God's Torah, and by, in general, Christian antisemitism and anti-Judaism? As Jesus said, true to Jewish ethics, "You will know them by their fruits" (Matt. 7:16).

I may interject here that once the New Testament is received as truly authoritative, the above word from Jesus becomes as integral to that authority as any other passage. This kind of word calls into question any blanket condemnation of the New Testament by Jews or others. But it also points to the problem Christians have of how to reconcile conflicting passages within their special scriptural authority.

The Jewish rejoinder to the Christian argument that the rightness of living requires the Christian faith is to turn that protestation against itself: The Christian disposition, particularly when it is attacking Jewish integrity, is revealed as morally reprehensible.

A final consideration of ostensible relevance under (b) is the trial and death of Jesus. (I say "of ostensible relevance" because of an argument I shall refer to later that the point is *not* relevant.) Volumes have been written and continue to appear upon this subject. To enter fully into it would require a book in itself.

As we bear in mind item (a) above, the only existential and practical motive for Jewish attention to the trial and death of Jesus is that Jews have suffered immeasurably because of the Christian ideology* of those events. The charge of Jewish culpability in Jesus' rejection and crucifixion has long been purveyed within Christian circles. Perhaps the most reveal-

---

*As used in this book, "ideology" refers primarily to the propagation of ideas in the service of a community's or collectivity's self-interest.

ing fact about the charge is its attempt to create an adversary relationship between "the Jews" and Jesus, this against the truth that Jesus was himself a faithful Jew. The attempt is thus not unlike such a proposition as "the Americans assassinated John F. Kennedy."

The Jewish rejoinder to the accusation tends to converge upon the findings of many historical scholars—including, be it carefully noted, many Christian scholars. According to that rejoinder, the accusation is saying a great deal more about itself than it is about reality. For in point of fact, the New Testament documents tendentiously alter historical truth by changing Roman responsibility for Jesus' death into Jewish responsibility. "Generations of Jews, throughout the Christian world, have been indiscriminately mulcted for a crime which neither they nor their ancestors committed. . . . If there can be found a grain of consolation for this perversion of justice, it is in the words of Jesus himself: 'Blessed are they which are persecuted for righteousness' sake: for theirs is the kingdom of heaven. Blessed are ye, when men shall revile you, and persecute you, and shall say all manner of evil against you falsely, for my sake. Rejoice, and be exceeding glad: for great is your reward in heaven' (Matt. 5:10–12)."[11]

At this point we are prompted to return to the word "ostensible" in the phrase, "the ostensible relevance of the trial and death of Jesus." From a Jewish moral perspective, but also from a more general or reasonable ("natural law") perspective, where is the legitimacy in continuing to concentrate upon the (alleged) blameworthiness of people respecting an event that took place centuries and centuries ago? Is it not unethical to impute culpability to Jews living today? Such an attempt is presuming the notion of collective guilt carried down from generation to generation. And is it not morally indefensible to keep alive in the here and now the guilt of persons who have been dead for two thousand years? The Vatican Council II declaration in 1965 on the church and the Jewish people, while asserting that what happened in Jesus' passion "cannot be blamed upon all the Jews then living, without distinction, nor upon the Jews of today," nevertheless insists that "authorities of the Jews and those who followed their lead pressed for the death of Christ." Furthermore, the council carefully eliminated an earlier draft proposal condemning the traditional accusation of deicide against Jews.*

*Perhaps of even greater significance to our subject as a whole, Vatican Council II identified the cross of Christ as "the fountain from which *every* grace flows" (emphasis added).

No one assumes any such stance respecting the actions of other ancient peoples, nor for that matter are Americans of our time at all troubled over much more recent collective behavior, such as the British treatment of the American colonists, or for that matter the Japanese attack upon the United States in 1941. The sins of the eighteenth-century British exercise very few people. *But neither do the possible virtues of the British of that time.*

What this implies is that any institutional or intergroup concentration today upon the subject of responsibility for Jesus' death, *not excluding a well-meaning insistence upon the innocence of Jews,* tends to play into the hands of those who have an ideological interest in keeping a certain pot boiling. For the real issue here has nothing to do with the guilt/innocence of Jews. It has to do with *the psychology of perpetuating a particular subject.* In the very moment of tacit acknowledgment that the question of responsibility for Jesus' death is to be treated as a living one rather than being made a deservedly dead one, things are ipso facto weighted upon the one side, namely, the traditional Christian side. This the Jewish side cannot tolerate, or ought not tolerate.

Minimally speaking, the legitimacy/illegitimacy of additional literature upon the subject of responsibility for Jesus' death is seen, accordingly, to be integral to the entire problematic of this book. Just why it is that the whole question did not long ago die out, or was not made to die out, must itself be viewed as of vital concern within the Jewish-Christian encounter.

In combination of items (a) and (b), the thesis may be offered that the Jewish people had/have nothing to do with Jesus' death, and accordingly that the topic is a non-question or, better, an immoral question. Jews will be in accord with the judgment of the National Conference of Catholic Bishops, "the Jewish people never were, nor are they now, guilty of the death of Christ."[12] This extremely simple way of putting the matter is intended to speak to extremely complicated historical-factual-moral data—not unlike the function of simple-sounding scientific theorems that may possess generalizing significance.

To conclude item (b): Some Jewish teachings, attitudes, and practices themselves appear to reflect a polemic response to Christian teachings and emphases. For example, the world-to-come and other eschatological teachings and concerns are often played down in Jewish quarters, some-thing that can well be, at least in part, a reaction against the great Christian concentration upon these things. In this same connection, the enterprise of theology has often been responded to negatively by Jews and Jewish thinkers, this in some measure against the dominating stress within Christian quarters upon correctness of doctrine and belief. Particularly in the Christian Scholastic tradition, life's problems become intellectualized. Again, some Jewish customs were actually relinquished because of their observance within the church (for instance, kneeling at prayer).

By and large, Christian emphases and teachings have never been greatly conditioned by the presence of the Jewish community (except in the early period of the church). Once more, the majority-minority status of the two groupings has to be kept in mind. Christian liturgy and many other practices are of course very considerably traceable to Judaism.

(c) The Jewish allowance for legitimacy within Christian faith and life has two facets. On the one hand, Christianity does fulfill a certain function in the world; on the other hand, Christians have often overcome their imperialisms and their trinitarian and other idolatries, and have practiced the love of neighbor and God.

(i) As far back as Moses Maimonides (1135–1204) the perception was forthcoming that the church helps bring true religion to the nations. For Maimonides, Christianity, while contaminated with idolatry, acknowledges the Torah even though it wrongly interprets it.[13] A like persuasion is found in the Jewish attitude to Islam. Maimonides wrote: "The teachings of Jesus the Nazarene and of the Ishmaelite [Muhammad] serve the divine purpose of preparing the way for the Messiah, who is sent to make the whole world perfect by worshipping God with one spirit, for they have spread the words of Scripture and the law of truth over the wide globe."[14] And for Franz Rosenzweig in our century, a miracle of the Christian church is that it disseminates the Torah of God to the world.

(ii) A totally cynical or denunciatory assessment of Christianity and Christian people founders upon the rock of more than occasional Christian goodness. Because this finding is proffered from within Jewish circles, and because Christian virtue vis-à-vis Jews is not anything new, the point is included at the present juncture rather than being reserved for chapter five on contemporary, inner Christian reform.

Christians are, with all human beings, part of the good creation of God. Jews are freely to accept and even to celebrate the *yetser tov*, the impulse for good, within the Christian soul.

Jews who read the New Testament, and are disturbed by its supersessionism and anti-Jewishness, find there as well many quite alternative and supplementary teachings:

> Blessed are those who hunger and thirst for righteousness, for they shall be satisfied.
> Blessed are the merciful, for they shall obtain mercy (Matt. 5:6–7).
> If you love me, you will keep my commandments (John 14:15).
> Love does no wrong to a neighbor . . . (Rom. 13:10).
> If I speak in the tongues of men and of angels, but have not love, I am a noisy gong or a clanging cymbal. . . . So faith, hope, love abide, these three; but the greatest of these is love (I Cor. 13:1, 13).
> Faith by itself, if it has no works, is dead (James 2:17).
> [According to God's promise,] we wait for new heavens and a new earth in which righteousness dwells (II Peter 3:13).
> We love, because he first loved us. If any one says, "I love God," and hates his brother, he is a liar; for he who does not love his brother whom he has seen, cannot love God whom he has not seen (I John 4:19–20).

Recent incarnation of the exalted moral and religious teachings of Christianity is found in the heroic and self-sacrificing acts of European Christians to save Jews during the Holocaust. Philip Hallie tells the story of Le Chambon, a French village, and of "how goodness happened there" in the deeds of Pastor André Trocmé and his congregants, who at mortal peril transformed their town into a sanctuary for Jews. They saved thousands of adults and children.[15] Much of the motivation for these and like actions was religious and (to the people involved) Christian: the command to love the neighbor and to love God in the neighbor.

Jews will point out that while it is true that the causes of the Jewish-Christian conflict fall much more upon the Christian side than upon the Jewish side, yet there are distinctive elements within American Christianity and within America as a whole that serve to offset this state of affairs. As Peter Grose writes, those "Americans who are willing to look see something of themselves in Israel. . . . Americans and Israelis are bonded together like no two other sovereign peoples."[16] Public opinion polls show repeatedly that Americans support Israel over her Arab foes by a five-to-one margin. In 1984 Congress voted overwhelmingly to establish a U.S.-Israel Free Trade Area. It is difficult to account for such realities and events apart from contributing positive influences from within the Christian community over two centuries and more. Regrettably, we cannot ignore contrasting and continuing Christian proclivities of an anti-Israel kind, nor can we forget the sorry record of the United States with regard to the rescue of Jews from Nazi Europe.[17]

Under the aegis of our pluralistic culture and open society Jews have been impressed by the more constructive aspects of Christian teaching and life. A free give and take between the two sides, often in friendship, is fostered. One consequence is Jewish recognition of redemptive moral qualities within Christianity. There is nothing within Jewish teaching, in principle, to keep Jews from dialogue with people of other faiths. Jews may learn from such encounters. They will not learn anything concerning their own faith-affirmations, but they may be enabled to understand their faith better and they may be aided in their human relationships. Theological and philosophical presuppositions are one thing; moral and political life is something else. It is in the latter respect that the Christian world may be viewed as having relevance to integrally Jewish thinking and decision-making. Christians help to bring important human challenges to Jews. From the standpoint of both Jewish self-interest and mutual self-interest, practical rapprochements ought to be worked out.

Of the three Jewish responses we have covered, (a) and (b) tend to be more conspicuous within one circle of the Jewish community, Orthodoxy, while (c) tends to be emphasized and turned to advantage within other Jewish circles: Reform, Conservative, and Reconstructionist. Orthodox Jews have much greater doubt of the rightness or efficacy of a dialogue with Christians than do non-Orthodox Jews. There are, of course, exceptions. Dominantly, Orthodoxy insists upon a limiting of conversation with Christians to secular topics. Other Jews are prepared to discuss a variety of subjects.

There appears to be considerable agreement across all Jewish lines upon a twofold affirmation that may serve to bring together the several reactions to Christianity reviewed in this chapter: Whatever is "bad" in Christianity arises out of misrepresentations of Judaism (e.g., that Judaism is a legalistic religion teaching self-salvation), out of extra-Jewish teachings and temptations, and out of human sin and untruthfulness. Whatever is "good" in Christianity is made possible by the church's having somehow kept alive essentially Jewish and humanity-serving norms and teachings. Accordingly, the overall historical relationship of the church to the Jewish people may be comprehended in and through the tension between this "badness" and this "goodness."

In conjunction with the "goodness" side, I may interpose that it is not correct to reduce the motivation of praiseworthy Christian moral behavior to the teaching and influence of Judaism alone. This is already hinted at within the second series of New Testament passages cited above. More will be said on this point in the final section of chapter five.

We have taken note of the Christian community's historic ambivalence toward Judaism. It is clear as well that the Jewish tradition is not without ambivalence toward Christianity. Eugene B. Borowitz epitomizes this point: Christianity "is a religion of ex-idolaters who worship God," but who came to that worship in a way that "retains overtones of idolatry."[18]

The traditional Jewish-Christian vis-à-vis boasts a long and tragic history. But the recent and contemporary relationship was never to undergo a more shattering crisis than in and through the cataclysm that began in 1933, with an impact that continues into today and will continue into tomorrow.

PART II

◆

Lineaments of Today's Meeting

3

♦

The Abomination

We come to the question of the Holocaust, an event profoundly apprehended by Arthur A. Cohen as the *tremendum*.[1]

As this question opens up, three caveats may be set down. First, it is unjust and untruthful to claim or to imply that Christian teaching and the Christian church were the sole creators of the Holocaust, and that the line from the New Testament through Christian history to the murder camps is a straight one and the only one that counts. Yosef Hayim Yerushalmi puts the matter well: "Even if we grant that Christian teaching was a necessary cause leading to the Holocaust, it was surely not a sufficient one."[2] Many extra-Christian and indeed anti-Christian influences helped produce the Holocaust. The various judgments expressed in this book upon the relation between Christianity and the Holocaust all presuppose that Christian teachings and Christian people do *not* bear all the guilt.

Second, it is unjust and untruthful to claim or to imply that there is no line from Christianity to the Holocaust. In light of Professor Yerushalmi's first statement, an additional comment of his gains that much more force: The church is not to be exonerated for its real and palpable guilt.[3] Emil L. Fackenheim writes, "the fact that Nazism was manifestly anti-Christian . . . is often used to avoid a Christian encounter with Auschwitz. But what if Nazi antisemitism was not *simply* anti-Christian but rather the nemesis of a bimillennial disease within Christianity itself, transmuted when Nazism turned against the Christian substance? In that case, Auschwitz would be *the* central theological event of this century not only for the Jewish but also for the Christian faith."[4]

Third, as Fackenheim insists, the horror of the Holocaust leaves but two choices: surrender to it or outrage. If it is so that to assume a tone of "clinical" detachment would be to commit a crime against the necessity of outrage, the same consequence would result from "self-indulgence" in a "writer's own mere feelings. The *facts* themselves are outrageous; it is *they* that must speak through our language. And this is possible only if one's feelings are subject to disciplined restraint. The language necessary, then, is one of sober, restrained, but at the same time unyielding outrage."[5]

I

In the congeries of events that comprises the Holocaust of the Jewish people (better termed *Ha'Shoah*, the Destruction), the German Nazis and their collaborators murdered six million Jews—at least twenty-five percent of whom were children—and smashed the lives of uncounted others. The tone-setters of the Holocaust are describable as "ordinary idealists." Their ideals "were torture and murder."[6] Two thirds of the murders were perpetrated after 1942, when the eventual defeat of Germany had already been assured. We could remind ourselves that idealists are not distinguished for practicality. But in this case the observation would be misleading: these idealists were devoted not to Germany but to killing Jews. At the latter point they were highly efficient and successful.

The end (*telos*) of the *Shoah* was to eradicate every Jew from the world: herein begins to appear the individuating incomparability of the event. In different terms, there was no longer to be a possibility of Jewish martyrdom or of the Jewish right to die in human ways. Of the *Muselmänner*, the anonymous mass of the camps, Primo Levi says that "one hesitates to call them living; one hesitates to call their death death."[7] The Nazis' "sacred mission" was to abolish the *being* of Jewishness. With the *Shoah* there is continuity and discontinuity respecting previous events. In the Inquisition, Christians burned Jewish bodies in order to redeem Jewish souls; in the Holocaust, the Christians of Nazi Germany burned Jewish bodies in order to redeem the world. Yet there is a "thread that spans the abyss": Strictly speaking, in the Christian view "Jews—and no one but Jews—should not exist at all."[8] As Fackenheim states, *existence* was now a capital crime—an unheard of proposition in the civilized world until the Holocaust.[9] But existence is a crime that only Jews commit: this Nazi dogma rules out any attempt to put the *Shoah* on a level with the persecutions of Gypsies or Slavs or others. (It is sometimes interposed that greater numbers of non-Jews than Jews were killed in the Europe of 1933–1945. This point confuses the issue of the nature and meaning of the *Shoah*, which is not a quantitative but a qualitative matter. Further, the point is extraneous to our subject. In our context of responsibility, the Holocaust is one with the *Shoah*, the destruction of European Jewry.)

Yet we have not yet reached the heart of the matter. The essential or ideal goal was not murder or destruction as such. It was to ensure that the Jews would destroy themselves through self-loathing. There was to be "self-transformation into the loathsome creature" that the Jew, according to Nazi ideology, had always been from birth and was trying to conceal, the parasitic vermin that was out to defile and vanquish good Aryan reality and the entire world. It was to be expected, therefore, that the Nazis would at once demand that the Jews keep themselves clean *and* make this impossible by depriving the victims of sanitary facilities, would guarantee dysentery for them *and* forbid them to relieve themselves except at the "correct" times. Jews were, in short, to be annihilated by their own excrement. The inner meaning of the *Shoah* is only grasped when the event is related to the truth that, in a phrase of Terence Des Pres, "the needs of the bowels are absolute." Jewish self-loathing was selected as the instrument to create an absolute wish for death.[10] In this connection, we know that wherever possible Jewish babies and children were killed in the presence or with the knowledge, and even with the "cooperation," of their mothers.

There is the undeniable datum that those who died in their own excrement included many non-Jews. Once the contention is accepted that the ultimate essence/meaning of the *Shoah* was to abolish the being of Jewishness by means of Jewish self-loathing and self-destruction, these non-Jewish deaths are to be received as a fateful consequence or accompaniment of the *Shoah's* essence/meaning. This is in no way to make non-Jewish suffering less terrible than Jewish suffering. For it is even possible to argue that the suffering of these uncounted others possessed a uniquely terrible aspect: they were in a sense "innocent" bystanders.

It is fitting to inquire: Who other than men possessed by the devil could devise the above arrangement? This is not to lessen their culpability but to give it a proper, inexorable frame of reference. At the very least, the freely chosen deeds of Nazi men succeeded in gaining identity with Satan himself, applying yet going beyond the punishments—hellfire could scarcely be worse—that had already been fabricated by an earlier collectivity of males, the Christian writers, priests, and theologians whose heirs the Nazis were.

The turning of human beings—the people of God and of the Torah—into excrement took place under the aegis of a country that represented the highest values of Christian and Western civilization: here the singularity and the lesson of the Holocaust are finally revealed. The new and true Israel could take its ultimate revenge upon the old and false Israel.

It follows that the only conquest of the *Shoah* from within its own parameters—the conquest, from outside, alone consisted in destroying the murderers—was the Jewish-human resolve, not explainable by either will power or natural impulse, "Although I now appear as the most contemptible thing possible, *I am not going to be revolted by myself.*" In the moment of this resolve, the German Nazi *Endlösung* was dispatched into its own self-destruction, into its own hell, even if the Jew (or non-Jew) making the declaration died an instant later.[11]

No consensus is more weighty on both sides of today's dialogue than the one that says: For the Jewish-Christian relation the Holocaust is a watershed without compare. That reality has revolutionized Jewish life and thought, and it has had a formidable impact, if a lesser one, upon Christian life and thought.

A number of Jews who endured the *Shoah* and somehow managed to survive are deeply offended when the event is treated as just one more instance, if an admittedly monstrous one, of Jewish and human suffering. Some Jewish scholars, particularly Orthodox ones, assume the latter, generalizing pose. Michael Wyschogrod is a noted example. Irving Greenberg, though Orthodox, stresses the singularity of the *Shoah* and its revolutionary, reorienting quality for Jews (and Christians). An avowal of the singularity of the Holocaust does not have to imply any denial of the uniqueness or the moral-historical significance of other events. On the contrary, Emil L. Fackenheim asserts that "to link Auschwitz with Hiroshima is not to deepen or widen one's concern with humanity and its future. It is to evade the import of Auschwitz *and Hiroshima* alike" (emphasis added).[12] In other words, those who reject special attention to the Holocaust as a unique or unprecedented* event are, in effect, rejecting the significance of the specific suffering of any and every people. They lose that significance within an abstraction labeled "suffering." Elie

---

*Fackenheim favors "unprecedented" over "unique" in speaking of the Holocaust; this, as he puts it, avoids taking the event out of history. The unprecedented character of the *Shoah* lay in its ideology and the objects of its intention: to ensure that there would not be a single Jew upon Planet Earth.

Wiesel writes, "It was Unamuno who said, 'When a Spaniard speaks of being in love, he speaks about all people being in love.' And when I speak of persecuted Jews, I also mean persecuted human beings everywhere."[13] (And the name for an insistence that events x, y, and z are of unique import but that the Holocaust is *not* of unique import is therefore: antisemitism.)

The Holocaust enters the purview of this book not alone through its transforming of the nature and quality of today's Jewish-Christian meeting, but as existential impulsion to continuing reflection, argument, and decision-making within the encounter itself. One way to come to terms with both these elements simultaneously is by means of exemplary representation of varying Jewish responses and varying Christian responses to the event, together with the interacting of these responses, sometimes in concord and sometimes in conflict. In and through such representation— it will be constitutive to chapters four and five—the affinities and the aversions of Jews and Christians that we have emphasized in chapters one and two will be granted further expression. Suffice it to mention here two points that comprise illustrative and specific links with the analysis to this juncture.

First, the moral asymmetry that characterizes the Jewish-Christian relation as a whole pervades the reality of the Holocaust and its aftermath. To Elie Wiesel's epigram, "If not all victims were Jews, all Jews were victims," Robert McAfee Brown responds: "Christians are called upon to say in addition, 'If not all Christians were killers, all killers were Christians.'" Wiesel has dubbed them "bad" Christians, yet Christians they were.[14] And they were consummating in bodily terms what had been the church's historic, ongoing spiritual genocide of the Jewish people, in the name of the Christian gospel and Christian salvation. This alone makes the Holocaust as much a Christian event as a Jewish event.

Second, on the one hand the dread status of victim threatened the core of Jewish identity: peopleness; and on the other hand the state of being victimizer ravaged the core of Christian identity: faith and faithfulness.

II

Three types of material and witness present themselves. First, there are responses to the Holocaust that do not directly bear upon our overall assignment—for example, that event's impact within purely Jewish ju-ridical or halakhic reflection or praxis. To concentrate upon inward-directed Jewish responses, or inward-directed Christian responses, would take us far afield and produce a different exposition. Second, some responses possess ultimate, if sometimes indirect, relevance to our specif-ic topic—for example, Jewish judgments and/or Christian judgments about Holocaust-God-human suffering. Third, certain responses have decisive, direct bearing upon our subject—for example, oral and written disputations over whether the Christian contribution to the Holocaust stemmed from things extrinsic or things intrinsic to the Christian faith. When Christians engage in anti-Jewish acts and thoughts, are they being "bad" Christians or "good" Christians?—quite another question from whether they are being "bad" human beings or "good" human beings.

Thus is a continuum involved. From the standpoint of this volume's interest, the more the different materials or testimonies approach the second and certainly the third of the three categories, the greater will be or ought to be our attention to them.

In keeping with the above distinctions, a word of counsel from Emil L. Fackenheim suggests a paradigm and point of departure. He refers to the differing priorities that Jews and Christians may or must have as they engage in dialogue in the aftermath of the Holocaust:

> For Christians, the first priority may be theological self-understanding. For Jews, it is, and after Auschwitz must be, simple safety for their children. [15]

This counsel's peculiar pertinence to our subject is evident in two re-spects. First, here is a Jew speaking to Christians as well as Jews. But, significantly, the very same or similar words could come from a post-Holocaust Christian speaking to Jews. However, in either case, and surely in the latter one, I should suggest that the needed "theological self-understanding" be explicitly made to encompass "theological and moral self-criticism." This suggestion is implemented in subsequent pages.

Second, Professor Fackenheim's counsel at once ties in with and au-thenticates the nature of the "two identities" we sketched in chapter one. Christianness means a faith; therefore, the theological enterprise is al-ways especially crucial, including its continuing reformation. Jewishness means peopleness; therefore, the safety of the children must be a pearl of greatest price.

Here I should like to enter two closely related provisos in the interest of averting rigidity. For one thing, a given priority does not enshrine a complete existential world. It stands at the forefront, and ought to do so. But it points to, and rests upon, other constituent factors. Thus, in the Christian case the essentiality of theological reformation is joined, as I just suggested, by that of needed moral reformation. For another thing, undue simplification is offset, on the one hand, by virtue of the faith factor that is associated with Jewishness and, on the other hand, by virtue of the human factor that is associated with Christianity: There is the need of *Jews* for theological self-understanding, and there is the need of *Christians* to keep their children safe.

In a word, the respective priorities in Emil Fackenheim's counsel are relative and comparative. Yet once all this is said, that counsel remains a profound description of the contemporary Jewish-Christian encounter in its normative dimension—under the force of the Holocaust. The counsel will be fundamental to much of the remainder of this book.

Those who are committed to a real-life Jewish-Christian encounter will not restrict expressions of fresh Jewish affirmation and praxis to Jewish voices alone. Christians as well are to be heard on that subject. And people so committed will not limit the expression of new movements within the church to Christian testimony. Jews as well are to be enabled to speak on that topic. Each of the witnesses can and will testify in behalf of the other side. Here, indeed, is found one of the more revolutionary and gladsome potentialities and developments within the new Jewish-Christian meeting: Christians speak for Jews, Jews speak for Christians.

In our two ensuing chapters the influence of Jewish responses and Christian responses to the *Shoah*, in their respective bearing upon today's meeting of Jews and Christians, is given an integral place. For any factoring out of the Holocaust from "the new Jewish stand" (chapter four) or from "commotion in the back of the church" (chapter five) would insert artificiality and even misrepresentation into the exposition and would detract from the truth of the revolutionary power of the *Shoah* within the contemporary relationship as a whole. "The Holocaust is not only an unprecedented event. It is also of an as yet unfathomable magnitude. It is world-historical."[16] However, the objective singularity of the *Shoah* has to be distinguished from, and cannot be confused with, required ways of responding to it. Once the Holocaust is treated within the overall fabric of moral and religious challenges to Jewish and Christian thinking and life, its lessons can then be responsibly applied—this in contrast to those exclusivist forms of fixation upon the *Shoah* that inhibit intelligent and constructive learning from it.

4

◆

The New Jewish Stand

I venture again a reminder of the selectivity and simplification that are the companions of brevity, here as everywhere in this book.

I

The wording "the new Jewish stand" is prompted by the contemporary Jewish community's determination to stand up to the world as Jews. This posture has, as we shall see, moral, political, and religious implications.

Fresh communal and personal self-affirmation on the part of today's American Jews has been occasioned through several factors. The development would not have come as far as it has were there not sustenance from religious and cultural pluralism, the influence of the distinctively American "voluntary principle," and the effectuating standard of religious liberty. Our century has witnessed the American religious community's change "from a world of mainstream and established Protestant hegemony and privilege to one that openly acknowledged pervasive pluralism."[1] It is adjudged that by the mid–1930s the Protestant era in the United States had already come to its end, i.e., the Protestant endeavor to turn America into a Christian nation was now in a state of decline.[2] In implementation of the ideal of religious pluralism—never to be confused with religious or ethical relativism—parties with differing faith-outlooks are helped to become understanding of and sympathetic to other views, while they nevertheless persevere in their own convictions. More specifically and more recently, the rising consciousness and self-legitimizing of many ethnic groups—"the new ethnicity"—has added environmental authorization and psychological and social support to the new Jewish identity. And then, in common with Jewish experience everywhere, there are lessons from the Holocaust.

In one of modern history's sublime reversals, the humiliating of the Jewish people in the *Shoah* has been succeeded by vigorous collective self-acceptance and self-assertion. The Holocaust created a Jewish resolve of "Never again!" In religious language, the commandment of *kiddush ha-Shem* (sanctification of the Name) is pursued—*not* replaced but instead fulfilled—by the commandment of *kiddush ha-hayyim* (sanctification through life).

Along with renewed and overt rejections of Christian supersessionism and anti-Jewishness, and amidst still-vivid memories of the *Shoah*—a terror yet being sustained in and through American exclusionist anti-semitism—Jewish identity is being reaffirmed in profoundly laic, moral, and political terms. After the Holocaust, any theology (together with human praxis as such) that is devoid of politics is seen to be emptied of validity and responsibility. The life of politics is the life of power, the capability of getting things done (in economic, social, religious, and other areas of culture). Hannah Arendt defines power as force combined with moral authority. If Lord Acton is correct that "power tends to corrupt and absolute power corrupts absolutely," it is just as true that powerlessness tends to destroy human life, and absolute powerlessness destroys human life absolutely. From the perspective of Judaism's historic-vocational struggle against idolatry, the challenge is how to maintain the rights and lives of human beings without falling into an evil absolutization of collective political identity. From the standpoint of Jewish ethics and Christian ethics alike, the absolutizing of a nation-state sets loose the demons of oppression, within as beyond national borders. Yet this eventuality does not negate the truth that, in principle, the nation-state is possessed of a legitimate, essential function: to protect human beings against the sins of others as of themselves, and to afford positive opportunities for living that are not otherwise available. Thus are we led into the subject of the State of Israel.

II

The reaffirmation of Jewishness as a laic-political reality entails, perforce, the reaffirmation of the Land.* "For seventy generations after the

*The capitalization here is intended to distinguish the Land of Israel (*Èretz Israel*) from other lands as well as from the general idea of land.

Roman destruction of Jerusalem . . . Jews gave voice to their passion for the land and to their profound and unshakable faith in their national restoration. . . . [The] hope for a return to the land of Israel helped the Jews endure all their sufferings."[3]

It is testified that the State of Israel "was actually established in the Warsaw Ghetto when Jews picked up arms and fought back literally to the last drop of blood."[4] Many of the widespread acts of Jewish resistance were those of martyrs, yet these deeds foreshadowed the return of Jewry to laic independence and even helped actualize that independence. The silence of Auschwitz "underlines the fact that hope without power is not a hopeful position in a world where power dominates, in a world that has seen all too clearly the price of powerlessness. It was this existential realization that made survivors of the *Shoah* such a crucial factor in bringing to an end two millennia of Jewish powerlessness."[5]

Zionism is the human liberation movement of the Jewish people. In the aftermath of the Holocaust there has taken place "the Jewish emergence from powerlessness."[6] This means commitment to the cause and the necessity of the State of Israel, reestablished as it was in 1948. It is impossible to overstate the influence of this new Jewish polity in counteracting the self-abnegation, and perhaps even self-hatred, amongst Jews that had issued from centuries· of oppression. Now, at last, "Jewish was beautiful."[7]

However, Israel is not merely a moral, psychological, and political necessity. Boasting as it does a very long history, it is also a blessing in its own right. The State of Israel is a singular Jewish celebration of life. This alone makes it a religious phenomenon, a hymn to the Creator of life. Thus, many Jews testify that when they set foot upon the soil of Israel their experience is one of having returned home, even though they may never before have visited the Land. How can this be? Christians sometimes report a comparable experience, although in their case the tie is strictly to their faith, through the "Holy Land" where Jesus walked and Christianity had its birth. With Jews the salient connection is to Jewishness—rather more like persons of Irish extraction who are fortunate enough (as I have been) to reach the Emerald Isle, perhaps for the first time ever. The Jewish experience of returning home to Israel manifests a collective laic consciousness that is very old. For Jews have lived uninterruptedly in the Land over several thousand years. As one rabbi has said, "for us Jews, Israel is our Jesus."

The abiding Jewish link to the Land disallows any attempt to make the

Holocaust *the* foundation of the State of Israel. And yet the two realities are bound together. We are met by a great paradox: The State of Israel has nothing to do with the Holocaust; Israel has everything to do with the Holocaust. The latter is true because apart from the Holocaust it is probable, historically speaking, that there would be no Israel today. That reality is not compensation for the Holocaust—how could there ever be compensation for such a horror?—yet Israel is an indispensable requirement for Jews in a ruthless, sinful world. We cannot repeat too often as an implacable lesson of the *Shoah* the essentiality of the State of Israel in Jewish survival. We must know, further, that there is no human refutation of the burning alive of the children of Auschwitz except the protecting of the children of today, in such a place as Jerusalem yet also in New York City and in Ethiopia. The fact remains, nonetheless, that the modern Zionist movement long preceded the Holocaust. It was more than a century ago, in 1882, that the young Russian Jewish "Lovers of Zion" issued their manifesto;[8] in 1896 that Theodor Herzl published his epochal essay *Der Judenstaat;* and in 1897 that the first world Zionist Congress, meeting in Basel, called for the creating of a Jewish state in Palestine. By the time Adolf Hitler had come to power, that state already existed in embryo form.

The roots and the integrity of Israel are entirely independent of the Holocaust. The Jewish people live in *Eretz Israel,* not by sufferance or historical catastrophe or merely as a place of refuge, but by right—a right that equals, or exceeds, that of any political sovereignty in the history of the planet. This suggests that the oft-heard formulation of Holocaust as "crucifixion" and State of Israel as "resurrection" has to be explained and qualified very carefully.

Once all the discontinuities between the *Shoah* and the State of Israel are responsibly maintained, there persists the stern continuity created by antisemitism, which was itself a primary impetus behind modern Zionism. And it is essential to remember as well that in the course of the rebirth of the State of Israel, antisemitism has itself been compounded. We are more than half way through a second Hundred Years' War, this time in the Middle East. For the Arab war against Jews was started back in the 1920s, and it has never lost sight of the single goal: to banish an independent Jewish presence from all of "Palestine."

It is important, in any case, to recall for the present context that in the most part the Tanak (Hebrew Bible) was not created in a time of Jewish powerlessness. Precisely in light of the fact that those documents are, according to Jewish tradition, linked to divine revelation, it is incorrect to use the overall biblical witness to support any assumption that human powerlessness is a precondition of God's life with a particular people. The most fervent advocate of the moral demands of the biblical prophets has to recognize that these demands entered into Jewish and human history after political sovereignty for the people of God was being achieved. Otherwise, such requirements could never have gained moral and social legitimacy and applicability.

The phenomena of Zionism and the State of Israel are classic evidences of the impossibility of conceiving a "spiritual" realm without a "material" realm, and a "material" realm without a "spiritual" realm. In this respect these movements embody the biblical refusal to separate the two realms (as they also contrast, therefore, with a great deal of Christian teaching). While Zionism could borrow its political theories from the world of modernity, its attachment to Palestine as the Jewish national homeland was inspired by the religion and tradition of Judaism.[9]

I referred in chapter three to a revolutionary development within the new Jewish-Christian meeting, the praxis of Christians speaking in representation of their Jewish partners, and of Jews speaking in representation of their Christian partners. A Christian biblical scholar epitomizes the Hebrew Bible's testimony: "There is an inseverable, eternal relationship among the People of Israel, The Land, and the God of Israel. . . . There is a 'chosen' people and a 'chosen' land: Israel's vocation is in terms of geography."[10] A Christian theologian writes: "In order to fulfill its redemptive vocation, the Jewish people need sovereignty—the power to regulate its life both internally and externally."[11] Thus are faith and geopolitical integrity linked dialectically: each reinforces the other. And a Christian historian ventures to sum up much Jewish (and some Christian) thinking upon the Zionist movement and a sovereign Israel, in the aftermath of the Holocaust: Zionism and the State of Israel

> constitute a renunciation of the "suffering servant" model that the people of Israel accepted for so many centuries. . . . Those conclusions that most Jews have reached, along with some Christians who have understood the absolute challenge that the Holocaust continues to represent, include: an insistence that the end of Jewish statelessness . . . is a responsible religious and political commitment; that forces of death and destruction—radical evil—must be resisted on behalf of life and a community's existence, even

if force and power are required for that resistance; that martyrdom can no longer be either the ideal religious or the responsible political method of responding to tyranny or other forms of evil; that peace and community must be the continual goal of our strivings, but not at the expense of a "sacrificial offering" of some one nation or people. It is time for the Jewish "return into history" with all the responsibilities and ambiguities—and mistakes—of power and decision-making that that entails, and all the courage that it requires.[12]

III

The Jewish community survived for nineteen hundred years while devoid of political autonomy. Accordingly, the sketch in the section just ended can hardly suggest that without Zionism and the State of Israel, Jews are deprived of their laic reality or heritage. Jewish cultural and social identity is multifaceted and abiding. Diaspora Jewishness is an ancient and living creation. Yet if it is so that the Holocaust shattered the notion of the Enlightenment and the Emancipation that Jews may find a peaceful and useful life in the Diaspora, is that judgment to apply categorically to Jewry in the America of today? Differently expressed, is there some integral place for "the chosen people in America"[13] or must that normative concept be abandoned? With aid from Stuart E. Rosenberg, Arnold M. Eisen, and others, let us turn to the American Diaspora.

Tolerance and the attractions of secular culture tend to drive Jews (as any people) toward assimilation; intolerance and fears of assimilation tend to drive them back to their tradition and to a certain isolation. "The ongoing tension between the two outlooks constitutes a basic dynamic in American Jewish life."[14] Through the centuries of the Christian era the Jewish community has lived out a basic dialectic of relative acculturation within the larger non-Jewish world combined with a striving to preserve Jewish identity. Paradoxically, the developing American experience has meant a partial easing of this condition but also its intensification. With respect to the intensification, Arnold M. Eisen says intriguing things about the socio-moral function of *silence* within the American Jewish community, as well as about the loss to the Jews of America of a distinctive language. ("English is a Christian language"—Cynthia Ozick.) Thus, the very phrase "chosen people" is misleading. As Eisen observes, "whereas 'the chosen people' makes chosenness an ascriptive status, a quality inherent in the people as such, the Hebrew reliance on active verbs such as 'God chose,' 'God loved,' 'God knew,' or 'God called' describes only what God did and indicates what Israel must do in response."[15]

On the one hand, the independence and the identity of Jewishness receive indirect validation and support through American social and political democracy, with special reference to religious voluntaryness and cultural pluralism. Yet there are, on the other hand, many temptations of assimilation and subjection to the "American way of life."

Amidst America's virtues and opportunities, the question persists, Wherein lies the distinctiveness of American Jewish life? Wherein is the meaning, the rationale of its manifest identity-in-diversity? It is observed that American Jews are at once a part of and apart from the world of America, and that as a way of protecting their Jewishness yet also their Americanness, they maintain a kind of "halfway covenant" with America.[16] But are Jewish distinctiveness and Jewish identity to be only "religious," or is there to be something more? This question is particularly challenging in the presence of the dominating social power of the Christian majority, which involves the still-menacing pressures and insecurities of antisemitism. For Christian anti-Judaism and anti-Jewishness have often been stimulated by the presence of a vital Judaism.

America's support of Jewishness has directed itself very considerably to the acceptance and advancement of Judaism. There is some irony in this, because Jewishness is so much more than another religion. It is surely the case that through the centuries the religion of Judaism has been foundational to Jewish survival. Yet were the only way to preserve Jewishness in America to be the honoring of religiousness, what ultimate consequences would this have for the broader and deeper matrix of Jewish laic integrity?

Varied lines of discourse are pertinent to the above problematic. We may single out five of many possible considerations.

(a) *A rapprochement of the profane and the sacred.* America has done strange things to people: "The creation of a cultural climate in which secularist and religious Jews would not only stop attacking or attempting to destroy one another but could even coalesce and merge—this could only happen to American Jews, because this was precisely what was transpiring in America itself. . . . [The] unique American process in which elements of secularism and religion are merging makes it difficult for Jews to remember that Jewishness and Judaism were once bitter enemies."[17]

The allusion is, of course, primarily to East European Jewry of the nineteenth and early twentieth centuries, which created secular Zionism.

One consequence here is a large measure of unity that would otherwise have been doubtful of achievement. However, while sometimes the best things in life are free, many times they carry a price tag. In the present instance, a compartmentalizing of life into secular and sacred has tended to develop—as when private or inward religio-ethnic preference manages to keep American culture at arm's length as being irrelevant or non-authoritative, but in the process helps American secularity to reign over the public roost.[18] (A comparable kind of dualism is a sight long familiar within much American Christian piety.) At the same time, since competing and conflictive group self-interest and wellbeing are integral to the American ethos and value system, to exclude expressions of peculiarly Jewish forms of self-interest and wellbeing would simply be antisemitism.

Rosenberg reports upon a "civil Judaism" that is "the truest common denominator of what most American Jews believe or practice" in the final decades of the twentieth century. "Civil Judaism" encompasses a commitment to the unity, distinctiveness, security, and welfare of the Jewish people, their tradition, and their community as a sacred value and mission; the cruciality of the State of Israel; endeavors in behalf of social justice and active participation in the wider society; and a theological pluralism that affirms individual conscience as final arbiter in religious belief and practice. These and other factors sustain and foster a "new group-conscious Jewish identity."[19]

(b) *Israel and the commitment of the American Diaspora.* Jews of the United States are caught up in at least two geographies, the promised land of the Hebrew Bible and America as land of promise. Jewish life in America fosters individual and communal meaning beyond the State of Israel, while Israel symbolizes and embodies special Jewish hope, dignity, and the will-to-survive. Dedication to Israel elevates American Jews above an unadventurous and complacent middle-class condition, and it does so in ways that count politically and morally.[20] (A parallel observation may be made respecting the dedication of American Christians to Israel.) However, it is essential to remember that it was under the aegis of the United States that Jewish fealty to Israel could gain such decisive effectiveness. Had American military and financial support and recognition not been forthcoming, and had the country been opposed to Israel, then, despite the presumed determination of a minority of Jews to sustain their Jewishness via explicit commitment to Israel, "the largest number would probably have put it aside as an impossible goal in America."[21]

Some Christian antisemites join other antisemites in accusing American Jews of a "dual loyalty" because of Israel. It is noteworthy that this charge is not made against other Americans who retain loyalties to, and lobby in behalf of, their ethnic homelands. Furthermore, national or laic commitment need not be blind or unthinking. Again, Christians do not always pay sufficient attention to the biblical prophets they claim to have inherited from Judaism. A convincedly prophetic vantage point will mean critical judgments upon the moral, political, and social idolatries of any country, not excluding the United States. But above all, as a recent editorial states, American Jews simply refuse to be made strangers in their own country—either through anti-Israeli acts or judgments on the part of others or by the political imposition of forms of religious (Christian) orthodoxy.[22]

(c) *A fresh acquiescence in the presence of Christianity.* The new self-acceptance and self-determination of Jews have some power to offset natural suspicions and negativism vis-à-vis Christians. Recent signs of Christian acceptance of Jewishness and Judaism (see chap. 5) have kindled a response among Jews, a much more positive Jewish stance toward Christianity and church people.

(d) *Jewish survival: The need to persevere upon two fronts.* The dream of most Jewish immigrants has been and is "to become Americans and to remain Jews."[23] In overall, practical terms this goal requires the twin thrusts of laic-ethnic integrity and religious belief and practice.

In the history of the Jewish people Jewishness has not always or necessarily fostered Judaism, and neither has Judaism always or necessarily fostered Jewishness. But in America, where secularism is wedded to religious values and religion is wedded to secularism, the ambience helps Jewishness and Judaism to be mutually supportive. At least, it helps more than it hinders. Thus can emerge the paradoxical interpenetration of a secularized Judaism and a religionized Jewishness. More positively expressed, American Jews will at once pour laic-ethnic content into their Judaism and find integral spiritual meaning in their Jewishness. However, they will do more than *find* spiritual meaning in Jewishness; they will also *assign* spiritual meaning to it. This latter gets underwritten in and through the tradition of Judaism, which has the power to offer meaning to the lives of Jews as persons.[24]

In the North America of recent years the observance of the Jewish religious tradition, devotion to Judaism, and Jewish education have all experienced revitalization.* Jewish academics fill significant roles in American higher education, although many of these people continue to lack strong allegiances to Judaism. There is a resurgence of intellectuality within the rabbinate, a reaffirmation of the rabbi's historic place as teacher and scholar. The contribution of Jews to cultural life and scientific advance is notably out of proportion to their numbers. In the 1980s scholarship and teaching in Jewish Studies as an autonomous discipline reached all-time highs, including appointments in Christian universities and theological schools, and extending to much work in Holocaust Studies. Jewish theology has gained new stature and significance since the Second Great War. That this last should be the case is traceable to a number of factors—not the least of which is the intellectual and practical need for symbolic procedures to sweep away "the previous identification of modern Judaism with rationalism."[25] In addition, we cannot overlook the outreach of a new, distinctively Jewish identity to encompass existential, critical reflection upon life's ultimate questions, including problems of the barbaric impulses within the human psyche and the phenomenon of cosmic evil. Theology ought not be the impropriation of Christianity. The pursuit of theological issues within the Jewish-Christian dialogue has also nurtured Jewish theology, while the latter in turn has been a strengthening force within the dialogue.

We have suggested that the attitude of the Jewish community as a whole toward America and its norms and opportunities is a necessarily dialectical one. Great care has to be taken lest Jewishness be overwhelmed and unduly acculturated, or that it be reduced to religiousness. But America is also to be celebrated as a place of unique freedom for Jews to be Jews, including the enhancement of the faith of Judaism.

(e) *Still small voices of prophecy*. Were we to omit a further factor, the present section of the analysis would be truncated. I say this despite the

---

*Perhaps as many as half of the some six million American Jews are affiliated with a synagogue. The approximate relative figures for affiliated Jews are: Conservative fifty percent (including Reconstructionist), Reform thirty percent, and Orthodox twenty percent. The Orthodox have the largest number of congregations but many of these are small. One promise of a bright future for right-wing Orthodoxy is the exceptionally high birth rate among Jews of that persuasion.

elusiveness and unobtrusiveness of the factor in question: the prophetic dimension.

One pertinent, illustrative point of departure here is the phenomenon and fate of the "Jewish vote" in the United States. True, American national elections of the 1980s probably mark the eclipse of whatever limited political balance-of-power role the Jewish community has played in the country as a whole. This development is linked to the demographic and industrial decline of the Northeast and to the smallness, even the shrinking size, of the American Jewish population. Presidential candidates will keep expressing support for the State of Israel, and the government will keep implementing that support, but this is largely explainable in the fact that the American people would not accept anything less (together with awareness of the country's self-interest). The survival and wellbeing of Israel are grounded, beyond the power and determination of Israel itself, upon the extra-Jewish resolve of the United States.

Having acknowledged the above state of affairs, we may yet make added reference to the outlook of the biblical prophets. The prophets were protagonists for justice and compassion, as have been their rabbinic successors and followers across the centuries. Are the voices of these people still being echoed? One possible answer may be hinted at in and through the following observation: "Jewish voting singularly among ethnic voting patterns has been supportive of political platforms frequently at odds with the economic interests of the relatively comfortable Jewish community."[26] This phenomenon was exemplified once more in the national election of 1984. Blacks chose overwhelmingly (ninety percent) the Mondale-Ferraro ticket: their perceived self-interest coincided with their vote. At the opposite end of the spectrum, white "born-again" Protestants supported almost as overwhelmingly (eighty-one percent) the other candidates, the Reagan-Bush ticket: here too perceived self-interest and voter choice coincided. Only a single identifiable grouping in the electorate showed a significant discrepancy between socio-economic self-interest and political decision-making: Jews. With them a notable hiatus appeared between the two factors. The Jewish vote was two-thirds for Mondale-Ferraro and one-third for Reagan-Bush, in the very face of the interests and middle-class identity and affluence of the majority of Jews. (A qualifying element here was Jewish fears of a threat, through Ronald Reagan, of the radical Christian right and of assaults upon the separation of church and state, but this element was of limited influence.[27]) It is pointed out that Jews live like Episcopalians and vote like Puerto Ricans. As one commentator wrote, the "most affluent ethnic group in America continues to vote its values instead of its interests."[28]

No insinuation is present here that the Democratic Party is the party of Amos, Isaiah, and Jeremiah. Yet we cannot ignore the wide agreement on opposing sides that one constitutive element in understanding the traditional link between American Jews and the Democratic Party is the Jewish concern for social justice.

Will Herberg argued that "the authentic Jew lives on two levels: as a responsible member of the historical community, and as a son of the covenant, a member of the trans-historical community of faith with which his destiny is inextricably linked. The authentic Jew is *in* this world, but never quite *of* it, never fully conformed or adjusted to the world in which he lives."[29] What Herberg said a quarter century ago is rather more descriptive of today's American Jews than of yesterday's. (It is descriptive as well of many Christians.) Stuart E. Rosenberg alludes to the possible collective-spiritual paradox of saving one's life through losing it: For some Jews, any movement within Judaism that merely accommodates itself to the parochial interests of individuals and groups in American culture "is destined to a long-term failure despite its short-term success. Only a religious commitment to Judaism based upon the historic faith and without regard to environmental factors can endure historically. And one must not expect that such intense devotion can be experienced by the largest number of Jews. In things of the spirit numbers do not count. In every age and place there was a 'saving remnant,' a small but dedicated minority of Jews, whose supreme religious commitments were responsible for the survival of the tradition."[30] Perhaps we may add: "and can today contribute thereby to the survival of the United States." For one way to advance the integrity and endurance of America is a social praxis that offsets self-serving Americanism.

Americanness, with all national collectivities, is peculiarly amenable to sins of idolatry. The singular way that Jewishness surmounts idolatry is through some kind of transcending of human absolutization. This possibility is expressible in theological terms: "Hear, O Israel: The Lord our God is one Lord" (Deut. 6:4). Within this frame of reference, a truly enduring contribution of Jewishness to the moral and spiritual health of America will center within the faith of Judaism. From a Protestant theologian comes a striking word. Paul Tillich did not believe "that a free society can be derived from any religion unless the religion has been profoundly influenced by the Jewish tradition."[31]

IV

The contemporary self-affirmation of Jews in the presence of other human beings and the societal realm extends as well to standing up before God and the domain of faith. This too is a discrete accompaniment and outcome of the *Shoah*. Completing a circle, we are led back to that event, now in a theological context. The Holocaust was the final horror and consummation of the oppression and antisemitism of Christendom. Yet if it is so that the power and place of God in the world do not excise human responsibility and blameworthiness, neither can the power and place of human sinfulness and freedom succeed in exonerating God. For the logic of Eliezer Berkovits appears impregnable: "God is responsible for having created a world in which man is free to make history."[32]

We may approach this matter with aid from the daring moral praxis of putting God "on trial" (cf. Elie Wiesel, *The Trial of God*. Wiesel's drama is set in the Ukraine of the seventeenth century; however, the playwright states that its genesis and motivation are the kingdom of night, the *Shoah*.[33]). Within the *Shoah* and its aftermath the awful question is posed of God's special accountability and even culpability. This question is tied fatefully to the very possibility of a revitalization of Judaism in a post-Holocaust time.

Certain personages are prepared to come forward as witnesses before the "trial of God." A few efforts to reckon with the existential enigma of God-Holocaust-suffering will be reported. Testimonies that do not positively reflect the new Jewish self-affirmation are not treated here. (These other views include the traditional persuasions that the sufferings of the Jewish people are simply [*sic*] due to their sins; that Jews are the special "suffering servants" of God; that in the *Shoah* there is the hiding of the divine face [*hester panim;* cf. Isa. 8:17]; and that the Holocaust is a mystery beyond all human comprehension and hence leaves no way to be withstood.)

(a) *The challenge to God as a paradoxical stroke for the acknowledgment of God.* Michael Chernick comments upon the verse, "I shall rebuke Him with my ways" (Job 13:15): "Challenging and questioning

God are not, for Judaism, unacceptable religious positions. Indeed, they imply that God's reality is taken most seriously. The act of challenging God can only be carried out by one who believes that God responds. For such a person, God is truly alive and capable of real and intimate relationships."[34] Thus, the moral praxis of the "trial of God" is itself not new. It is rooted in pre-Holocaust Judaism, particularly in Hasidism, and is traceable ultimately to the age-old plaint of Abraham, "Shall not the Judge of all the earth do right?" (Gen. 18:25). However, with the *Shoah* this genre of theological vis-à-vis gained fresh advocacy. By contrast, any eventuality of the "trial of God" had not, so far as I know, ever received autonomous expression in Christian circles until it was introduced therein via the post-Holocaust Jewish-Christian dialogue.* In Wiesel's *Trial of God* a certain symbolic shift may, accordingly, inhere in the identity of the character who is privy to the terrible secret that the individual who agrees to serve as God's defense attorney is in fact Satan. The one who knows this is a Christian woman. The Christian psyche may be here apprehended as confronting itself at a well-nigh unbearable level: Does not God bear culpability, along with the Christian world, for the Christian dispensation that issued in the *Shoah?*

Hence it is possible to enter a double indictment, the two sides of which involve the single and singular moral problem of the divine responsibility-foreknowledge:

(i) Expressed within a strictly Jewish frame of reference, God ought to have realized that the covenant with Israel, making her "a kingdom of priests and a holy nation," a chosen light to the peoples of the world (Exod. 19:6; Isa. 42:6), would culminate in the death camps—in, to use the Nazis' own terminology, "the ultimate solution to the Jewish question" (*die Endlösung der Judenfrage*). If the divine demands upon a people are only going to ensure the horror of endless suffering and destruction, do not those demands cease to be divine and become demonic? Moreover, do they not ironically and inherently contradict one intrinsic dimension of the covenant itself, which stipulates that by being faithful to the Torah of God, Israel will *live* (Lev. 18:5)?

(ii) Expressed within a strictly Christian frame of reference, God ought to have realized that the Incarnation-Crucifixion-Resurrection was going to be fabricated into a Christian supersessionism and triumphalism that

---

*On a Christian view, the possibility has yet always obtained of interpreting the person of Jesus as a special "trial of God."

would surely make for the identical dire consequence of Jewish destruction. The two counts of the indictment converge in the one question: What is the moral relation of the divine initiative and providence to human history, human responsibility, human fate?

To be sure, there is no sense at all in which Jews are to construe the events taught by Christianity in the way that Christians believe them. However, this does not annul Jewish reflection upon the potential relevance of Christianity here, simply because Jewish tradition has always allowed a possible role for Christianity in the divine economy, e.g., the church's disseminating of Torah amongst the nations. At the very least, in view of the truth that it is the same God who unites (and separates) Jews and Christians, the issue here is seen as integral to today's Jewish-Christian encounter. Within the courtroom of the "trial of God" Jews and Christians are facing God, but they are also facing one another.

As the trial proceeds, the theological lamentations of Elie Wiesel and others are heard. In Wiesel's *A Beggar in Jerusalem* a certain *zaddik* agonizes: "It is easy to die for You, easier than to live with You, for You, in this universe both blessed and cursed, in which malediction, like everything else, bears Your seal."[35] Such lamentations suggest the eventuality that to bring to trial "the hiding God of history" (Eliezer Berkovits) may be the one hope left, in the shadow of the kingdom of night, for an honest and authentic witness to God, for sanctifying the Name of God—at least once it is agreed that the way "God proves himself holy" is "by righteousness" (Isa. 5:16).

The traditional rejoinder is given voice—the attorney for the defense speaks—that humankind exists for the service of God.[36] But, so it is also held, the true service of God must involve questioning, criticizing, and even castigating God—for strictly moral reasons. Otherwise, why has God endowed humankind with a moral sense and moral responsibility?

(b) *Eclipse of God, death of God*. For many Jews within as beyond the camps of death, the *Shoah* constituted ultimate proof of the moral impossibility of faith, since it proved once and for all the absence or enmity or immorality or non-existence of God.

To take a position such as that of Richard L. Rubenstein[37] is to conclude that after 1933–1945 there remains no Judaism in any effectually traditional understanding. That is to say, 1933–1945 is the end of Jewish hope *in the sense of Jewish religious hope*. (How can there be Judaism once hope in the God of history is gone?) From this standpoint, the all-decisive implication of 1933–1945 is that Jewishness gains essential regnancy over

traditional faith. The received God of Judaism is rejected as either un-
worthy or impotent, or both. Yet, paradoxically, this is not the end of
religion, of the search for meaning. "It is precisely because human existence is tragic, ultimately hopeless, and without meaning," that we must
all the more "treasure our religious community. . . . If all we have is one
another, then assuredly we need one another more than ever."[38] And
Jews are called to devote themselves to such strictly human creations as
the State of Israel.* Thus is a distinctively Jewish stand still being taken.

(c) *The command to live, and beyond that command: Faith as absolutely
fragile.* Emil L. Fackenheim is widely known for his plea that no post-
humous victory be handed to Adolf Hitler through the abdicating of
Jewish faith, hope, and life. Traditional Judaism sustains 613 commandments. Out of the murder camps came a 614th: the command to
Jews to survive, and to survive as Jews.[39] However, while his affirmation
of God contrasts with Rubenstein's denial of God, Fackenheim has turned
away from any theological attempt "to show that nothing unprecedented
could call into question the Jewish faith" itself. It is just not true that
Jewish faith is "essentially immune to all 'secular' events between Sinai
and the Messianic days."[40] Fackenheim has contended for some years that
in contrast to the Christian eschatological expectation, the Jewish expectation is "at least in part falsifiable by future history. . . . After
Auschwitz, it is a major question whether the Messianic faith is not
already falsified—whether a Messiah who could come, and yet at Auschwitz did not come,† has not become a religious impossibility."[41] If it is so,

---

*Is not the presence of the State of Israel interpretable in radically different ways? Israel
may be construed as a wholly human creation. But it may also be received as an effectuation
of the divine promise. Even granted that no consolation is possible for the horror of the
Holocaust, the fact is that those who are known as the people of God do endure. Israel in its
corporate integrity was not only saved from destruction but was given political sovereignty.
One of my philosophic-historical presuppositions is that any and all events are open to
interpretation in any and all ways, e.g., non-religiously and religiously, non-theologically
and theologically.

†One *could* respond here that the coming of a Messiah to deliver the Jews of Auschwitz and
the other murder centers was indeed a religious impossibility because it was already in fact a
physical impossibility, and hence that the expectation of any such Messiah is superstition (an
issue quite unrelated to the Holocaust). It is clear that the world has not been arranged along
lines of that form of intervention. The remnant of Jews was saved by the troops of the Allied
nations (which included the forces of the Soviet Union). To identify these armies as
"messianic" would rather make for a confusion of categories. But yet this is not to say that
God did not *use* these soldiers for his/her own purposes. From the standpoint of faith in
God, any denial of the latter utilization would itself be an exercise in "superstition" (having
to do with an incorrect or simplistic hermeneutic of ultimate cause-and-effect).

Fackenheim continues in *To Mend the World*, that the Holocaust is (as Irving Greenberg has it) a qualitatively and absolutely unique and radical "countertestimony" to both Judaism and Christianity, how could such a thing as a "commandment" ever be capable of withstanding the destructive implications of the *Shoah* for faith? "Must not Jewish and Christian faith . . . be either, after all, *absolutely* immune to *all* threats or else destroyed by *this* threat?" What is to be the life-and-death outcome once we grant, as we must, that Jewish faith, in the presence of *this* Event, the *Shoah*, is *not* immune to all experiential events? This latter, Fackenheim testifies, has become for him "the central question of all Jewish and indeed all 'post-Holocaust' thought, so much so that all else depends on how one grapples with it."[42]

"The task is *Tikkun Olam*, to mend the world." This "ontological possibility" (to be sure, a necessarily fragmentary one) obtains only if it can call upon an "ontic reality." But this latter has come to us. For, astonishingly, there was *within the Holocaust itself* a Jewish *Tikkun:* Some, a few, did say No. They did not succumb. This "enormous, nay, world-historical truth is the rock on which rests any authentic Jewish future, and any authentic future Jewish identity. . . . [This] ontological Ultimate—a *novum* of inexhaustible wonder, just as the Holocaust itself is a *novum* of inexhaustible horror—is the sole basis, now and henceforth, of . . . Jewish existence, whether religious or secular."[43] *I am not going to be revolted by myself.*

The absolute fragility of faith is held together with the delivering God of Judaism. Witness the State of Israel, which is of itself the *Tikkun*.[44] A telling contrast to viewpoint (b) above is realized. For Emil L. Fackenheim the God of human history is not lost. "God and History are not divorced. Israel and God are not torn asunder."[45]

(d) *Moment faith and the voluntary covenant.* An allied endeavor to grapple with the assault upon Jewish faith by the events of history is that of Irving Greenberg, who readily grants that "the cruelty and the killing raise the question whether even those who believe after such an event dare to talk about God who loves and cares without making a mockery of those who suffered."[46]

Greenberg affirms a radically dialectical position that seeks to take with full seriousness both a dethroning of the God of history and an upholding of the God of history. He pleads for a "moment faith." Before the fact of the *Shoah*, "there are times when faith is overcome. Buber has spoken of 'moment gods': God is known only at the moment when Presence and awareness are fused in vital life. . . . We now have to speak of 'moment faiths,' moments when Redeemer and vision of redemption are present, interspersed with times when the flames and smoke of the burning children blot out faith—though it flickers again." One powerful incentive to a renewal of faith is the Holocaust itself, for is not that event the sort of abyss into which self-sufficient, secular humankind falls when it trusts in itself rather than in God? To put God to death is to erect idols in the place of God. It is to guarantee destructiveness. Here is the demonry of modernity. Yet Greenberg knows only too well, with Fackenheim, the fragility in our time of faith in the true God. "To let Auschwitz overwhelm Jerusalem is to lie (i.e., to speak a truth out of its appropriate moment); and to let Jerusalem deny Auschwitz is to lie for the same reason. . . . [In] a striking talmudic interpretation, the rabbis say that Daniel and Jeremiah refused to speak of God as awesome or powerful any longer in light of the destruction of the Temple."[47] Must there not be a parallel refusal after the *Shoah?* This question leads into Irving Greenberg's persuasion of a "voluntary covenant."

From experience of the *Shoah* we know that God does not intervene, despite the extremity of his people (though God suffers and makes himself vulnerable within and through that very non-intervention). Instead, human beings are the responsible parties now, they are on their own—not that they are to continue to suffer or to inflict suffering, but that they are to fight against suffering and establish justice, a struggle that requires, among other things, the responsible utilization of power and the redistribution of power (and therefore many hazards, temptations, and compromises).

To *demand* that Jews today follow Torah and covenant is a heteronomous impossibility after the *Shoah.* Yet Jews do not have to abdicate Torah and covenant out of despair or autonomous self-assertion. The alternative to heteronomy and autonomy is a free acceptance of theonomy, a wholly voluntary readiness to persevere with aid from the liberating mantle of Torah, to do so in other-directed service and self-fulfillment and accordingly in joy and laughter. A consequence of this potential achievement is that any and all invidious comparisons between religious and non-religious people are put to shame. Where freedom reigns, there is indivisibility and human solidarity. For it is through the sanctifying of human life as such (*kiddush ha-hayyim*), through existence in the world, through *holy secularity,* that the divine Name is sanctified (*kiddush ha-Shem*).[48] A voluntary covenant for today is the integral culmination of Irving Greenberg's general Jewish philosophy of history, which contains three major phases: the biblical-prophetic age, initiated in the Exodus and Sinai, with a highly manifest God as, so to speak, "senior partner" and humankind as "junior partner" in the covenant; the rabbinic age, initiated in the destruction of the Temple, with humankind and a less manifest God as more or less equal partners; and the third cycle, initiated in the *Shoah* and the rebirth of the State of Israel, with God as a much more hidden and reserved "junior partner" and humankind now as "senior partner."[49]

"Many are shocked by the suggestion that the Holocaust smashed the covenant. . . . They fail to understand that this broken covenant is even more powerful having been renewed by the Jewish people and its covenant partner. Faith based on the expectation of guaranteed succor is conditional, vulnerable to the shattering blows of history. Faith and covenant built again after the Holocaust is proof against the fires of hell."[50]

Through the persuasion that the Jewish community is to take entire responsibility for its life and future, the new Jewish stand reaches a climactic point. Yet this is not humanist or idealist self-sufficiency. It is a contemporary fruition of the abiding covenant with the living God.

(e) *Beyond the Holocaust, beyond the trial and the death of God.* The specter of the *Shoah* hangs over all the views we have surveyed. Noteworthy signs of change are represented in a passage from Eugene B. Borowitz, words that reflect the quality of so much Jewish existence in today's America: "Not long ago many writers were saying that our entire Jewish way of life must now be rebuilt around the Holocaust. With most of us day by day finding normality the basic condition of our lives, that older view seems faulty. Frightful disasters occur and dreadful horrors are still regularly perpetrated. We must never be blind to the hells about us or to the potential of their occurrence. But our lives are very far from a recapitulation of Auschwitz; they are not even greatly illuminated by its uniqueness."[51]

Is there a bridge between the new life that, blessedly, is "very far" from the *Shoah* and the necessitated, obligational memory of that event?

For increasing numbers of Jews, there endures upon the other side of the unredeemedness of the world—an unredeemedness that surely demands the rejection of one or another (failed and/or false) messiah—the hidden yet historical God who, despite all, stays faithful to the promise that the Age of the Messiah will be a time of justice, of peace, of safety for the children. The *Shoah* is still apprehended in all its unparalleled horror. Yet under the power of the Jewish will-to-live and by virtue of new celebrations of life, all in accord with age-old Jewish experience and a massive historical memory of sublime as well as baneful things, the banishment of the horror is begun. Moreover, beyond the celebration of historical life stands a dimension of existence that transforms history itself. (We referred in chapter two to the Christian appropriation of eschatology.) The resurrection of the dead was a Jewish affirmation well before Christianity began, although the conviction is by no means universal among Jews of today.[52] Irving Greenberg declares, in a kind of Kantian application, that "the moral necessity of a world to come, and even of resurrection, arises powerfully out of the encounter with the Holocaust."[53] In the resurrection may be embodied the salvation of the hopeless ones, the despairing ones, the murdered ones, the nameless ones, the little ones—those who are for now totally pitiful and destroyed and lost. Yet this incredibility, this transformation remains possible only if—in Abraham Joshua Heschel's recapitulating of the prophetic pathos— the voice of the sovereign Lord of the promises is "a voice of grief, a voice of weeping."[54] The unmitigated horror of the *Shoah* is mitigated, not by human forgetfulness or worldly success, but only by the tears of God.*

V

What may the Jewish people find themselves called tangibly to do concerning their faith of Judaism in the epoch after the Holocaust? Actual and potential responses to this question are legion. I limit myself to just one such response, and this in brief form, the contemporary "witness and mission" of Judaism,[55] which raises the quite different though related question of Jewish conversionism. I do this on several grounds. The main reason is that the development is exemplary of the new Jewish stand.

*The shift here to a religious way of writing is for purposes of consonance with the religious character of the point of view being described. This method surfaces in later pages as well. See preface for a brief methodological note on the appropriateness of differing forms of literary exposition within a single book.

Second, the movement constitutes a notable, if not absolute, reversal within the traditional Jewish-Christian relationship. Third, it adds depth and nuance to our special concern with the American situation and the country's heritage of freedom for religion. Last, the development is marked with special poignancy, before the fact of the *Shoah*. We have been attending to the crisis-fragility-denouement of Jewish faith in the aftermath of that event. In existential awareness of the lessons of the *Shoah*, Daniel Polish asks whether Jews dare make witness at all: May such witnessing only seal the fate of generations yet unborn?[56] Yet there is an equally unyielding, or more unyielding, fact: The Jewish people do not give up, Israel does not give up. To Martin A. Cohen, the *Shoah* "has left little doubt that the Jew's best option is to reconcile himself with his mission, and to proclaim openly, as the prophet Jonah was constrained to do, 'I am a Hebrew and I serve the Lord' (Jon. 1:9)."[57]

"Through the ages the concepts of Israel's chosenness and mission have remained central in its theology. Without both, the distinctive dimensions of other theological affirmations in Judaism, including revelation, the covenant, the messianic age and even God, are immeasurably compromised."[58] The biblical and talmudic traditions alike propound the duty of Jews to share the essential teachings of their faith with the outside world. In the Graeco-Roman period the Jewish people engaged in active missionary work.[59] The dissipation of this activity was due to many factors. In Christian Europe the authorities forbade it. In chapter two we noted the internalizing bent of Judaism, its directedness in the first instance to the Jewish community. Converts to Judaism have of course always been accepted, though never without the voicing of serious caveats to them concerning the special obligations of the practicing Jew and the hazards of Jewishness in a world that is hostile.

The American situation manifests interesting paradoxes. For example, on the one hand, there is the fact of attrition within the Jewish community. A basic problem respecting the relative-numerical future of Jews is that their birth rate is below the national average. (In 1948 Jews comprised more than three percent of the American population; today they are less than two and a half percent. "If the present trend is not soon reversed, American Jewry will effectively lose a million people, or perhaps even more, by the end of the century."[60]) On the other hand, whatever the Jewish position is to be on the issue of conversionism, gentiles do become Jews. More than 100,000 of today's American Jews were not born Jewish. Each year over 2,500 people convert to Judaism in the United States. Approximately eighty percent of these are women who are marrying Jewish men and establishing Jewish homes.[61] However, perhaps as many as half of all Jews who marry wed non-Jews.

In keeping with the freedom of and for religion that characterizes the United States, missionaries are all over the place, in behalf of all kinds of religions. Ought the advocacy of Judaism remain an exception? Is the Jewish "mission" to remain "non-missionary"? Alternatively, what specific motivations and purposes may lie behind a possible contemporary Jewish missionary effort?

Everyone knows that the traditional Christian idea of saving souls from perdition or for eternal life through faith in Jesus Christ or even through faith in God has no meaning to Jews. However, this does not exclude a factor that is definitely outer-directed: a collective desire to share the blessings and values of Judaism. Martin A. Cohen emphasizes the restless Jewish struggle to universalize the Wilderness Ethic. The sacred task of post-*Shoah* Jews, he contends, is to help eradicate the manifold deterrents to the full humanization of the species.[62] Second, there is an inner-directed factor: the obligation to sustain and prosper the people Israel. Within this rubric can be placed the program of the Lubavitch community to "convert" Jews into faithful practitioners of the *mitzvot*. Under this same general heading belongs the fact that the Jewish community is continually being subjected, indirectly and directly, to conversionism from the majority Christian side, and must act to defend its own integrity.

The two elements mentioned are by no means mutually exclusive; they cannot be finally separated. A third consideration is suggested in words from Ben Zion Bokser: "The stress in the Jewish concept of religious witness is on the general illumination of people toward the recognition of the universal sovereignty of God and the primacy of the moral order."[63] Here the obligation to witness, while sustaining the Jewish mission, may actually inhibit discrete missionary or conversionist endeavor, since people can presumably be brought to honor God's presence and the moral order without necessarily being or becoming Jews. However, there is yet present here a Jewish obligation to other human beings and to God. As long as that duty is insisted upon, the door to conversions to Judaism is anything but closed.

It is noteworthy that the new Jewish missionary thrust is largely associated with the Reform movement. In 1983 the Union of American Hebrew Congregations created a "Commission on Reform Jewish Outreach," with the purpose of establishing programs "to encourage both the non-Jewish parents in mixed marriages and their children, along with the 'unchurched,' to convert to Judaism—to become Jews by choice." (In the same year the Central Conference of American Rabbis resolved that non-converted spouses among Reform families who wished to adhere to Jewish religious practices, even though not formally converting, would be looked upon as Jews.) Attention was to be directed to religiously non-committed people. Rabbi Rosenberg observes that not since the Pharisee period has such a missionary view taken hold within the Jewish community. In the post–1967 era, the American Jew was embarking upon "a new-style emancipation: one that would discard the self-alienating attitudes of the older emancipation" in Western Europe "and the more recent one in America itself. . . . [In] a most paradoxical way, his earlier troubled concern with what America thought of him as a Jew, his once poignant need to be sustained from the outside in his acceptance of inner Jewish values, have been largely responsible for his new assurance, at long last, that now, if he wills it—not others—he is free to be himself in a newer and freer America."[64]

One ironic complication in the contemporary Jewish mission is that discrete efforts within the Reform movement to share Judaism and to ensure Jewish survival are rejected by those Orthodox Jews who question the legitimacy of Reform (and Conservative) Judaism as well as by some secular-minded Jews who see in the program a violation of American norms of pluralism and mutual respect. Representatives of Orthodoxy were particularly scandalized by recent resolves within the Reform camp (as to some extent among Conservative Jews) to consider as a Jew a child of a non-Jewish mother and Jewish father (provided that such is the intention of the parents).

An additional complication cannot be avoided. Should the Jewish community wish to engage in a missionary outreach that will inevitably address Christians, does equality of partnership in the dialogue dictate that Jews accept the right of the church to a missionary outreach that inevitably addresses Jews? Or does this matter sustain some kind of asymmetry? (This problem receives further attention in the next chapter.)

Today's challenge of the Jewish witness and mission, including the current debate over a policy in support of active conversionism, points up the question of whether the new Jewish stand has lessons primarily for Jews or whether it has implications for human life beyond the Jewish community.

It has been observed that the 1960s and 1970s were distinguished by a "historic decision of the world Jewish community to turn toward survivalism as the basic policy."[65] The challenge of the 1980s and on into the twenty-first century is: Upon the prerequisite foundation of Jewish survival, what uniquely Jewish contributions are to be made to the country and to humankind that will at the same time avoid the acculturationism that wastes Jewish integrity and compromises Jewish identity? Jews need to be reminded, writes Arthur A. Cohen, "that there is more to being Jewish than having the protection of American law and the solace of the beleaguered Jewish community of Israel."[66] The integrity of North American Jewry—in theological terms, its chosenness—does not derive solely from either the present reality of the State of Israel or the past reality of the *Shoah*. That integrity is sustained as well in and through this continent's life of today, its particular historical responsibilities and opportunities. It seems to me that Jews *are reminding themselves* of Cohen's point. This is the whole meaning of the new Jewish stand.

A postscript to the new Jewish stand. I noted in chapter two the understandable disregard of Jesus of Nazareth within Jewry insofar as that figure has been appropriated by the church. The continuing confiscation of Jesus in the Christian community is the basic psychological and material obstacle to a positive Jewish attitude to or rediscovery of Jesus. This obstacle is kept in place by traditional Christian triumphalist ideology.

A prime contemporary example of such triumphalism and of the inveterate Christian effort to sequestrate Jesus is a study by an American evangelical, Donald A. Hagner, titled *The Jewish Reclamation of Jesus*. Not unexpectedly, Hagner falls into traditional Christian ideology. He maintains that today's Jewish reappropriation of Jesus is disingenuous because Jews are all along continuing to reject in Jesus "their own Messiah." Hagner strives to hammer a wedge between Jesus and Torah and to make the New Testament innocent of all antisemitism. Almost unbelievably, he accuses Jewish scholars of taking from the Gospels only what accords with their views. In other words, the Jew gets condemned for not reading the New Testament as a Christian reads it. Hagner's charges concerning the Jewish reappropriation of Jesus are relentlessly *parti pris*—not unlike the utilization of a thief's criterion respecting who owns the property he has stolen. There is no way to separate Hagner's fervent, supersessionist anti-Judaism from antisemitism. In a fashion reminiscent of timeworn antisemitic invective, he finds Jews "more and more aggressive" in their reclamation of Jesus.[67]

The entire notion that Jesus is somehow the possession of the Christian church and that Jews today are somehow "reclaiming" him is only made possible by the centuries-old Christian effort to take Jesus away from his own people. What conceivable meaning could there be in Jews "reclaiming" someone who is already their own? The reason that Jews have traditionally said relatively little about Jesus (in contrast to, say, Hillel) is considerably due to Christianity. The most that "the Jewish reclamation of Jesus" can mean is his restoration to his people in deliverance from his captivity by the church.

The Christian community will begin to merit its dedication to Jesus only when, paradoxically, it stops claiming him as a Christian possession. In the measure that Jesus is received as the fully Jewish human being he was—an identity that is insisted upon, not alone by the Jewish community but by increasing numbers of Christians today—the substantive and principled barrier to his reappropriation by Jewry will be overridden. It is noteworthy that, in contrast to the situation in North America with its dominating Christian majority, such reappropriation has in fact been taking place in the State of Israel, where Jewish life has at last been liberated from Christian hegemony.[68] Jesus of Nazareth may yet come into his own as a son of Israel and be restored to full dignity—in and through his own people.

5

◆

Commotion in the
Back of the Church

We now move from a Jewish frame of reference to a Christian one. Eugene B. Borowitz contends that for American Jews the Holocaust is largely past history. Ought such a stance be adopted by American Christians? This is another way of asking: Have Christians come to terms with those dimensions of Christian teaching that helped bring about the Holocaust and serve to perpetuate antisemitism?

Perspective for dealing with these questions may be garnered through study of current struggles within the Christian community. The first portion of the chapter will introduce its theme; the remaining section will enter more into specifics.

I

The chapter title requires a little commentary.

It is as though certain disturbances have started to break out in the rear pews of church services and meetings here and there. The occupants of the great body of middle and front seats naturally wish to be left alone to concentrate upon the cross at the altar or the Host there or Scripture or the preacher in the pulpit or the sacred hymns. They want to receive without interruption or interference the pure and saving Word of God. Yet now the commotion in the rear is distracting and bothering them. And some of them are impelled to turn and see just what is going on.

Who are the troublemakers and what are they trying to do? Is it not illegal to cause a disorder at public worship? (Look there, a few of the people are even wearing clerical garb.) Now their disruption of the service of God is extending to the display of a string of placards: "John

8:44 is the road to Auschwitz." "The Catholic Church never excommuni-
cated Adolf Hitler." "Jewish children were burned alive." "Jesus was a
Jew." "God is on trial." "Christianity is on trial." "Power to the Jewish
people!"

Much irony is manifest in this book. One ironic aspect of the commotion in the back of the church is that many of the agitators turn out to be
academicians, of all people. Ordinarily, scholars do not go around upsetting the social or religious status quo. This is how they can be accepted by
their world. But the wording of one placard proves to represent the
central thesis of a lengthy scholarly and historical study by a Christian
theologian.[1] The wording reads, "Anti-Judaism and antisemitism are the
left hand of Christology."*

A fact obtrudes: The finding that the traditional Christian attitude to
Jews and Judaism helped make the Abomination possible and perhaps
even inevitable has become a truism of recent historical scholarship. Its
being a truism makes unnecessary our elaborating upon it here. However, a really important consideration—anything but a truism or redun-
dancy—is that *Christian* scholars are involved in that finding along with
Jewish and other scholars. This provides a significant counterbalance to
unalloyed cynicism respecting Christians and the Christian church. What
these scholars are saying is inspirationally and educationally decisive for
the commotion that is upsetting divine worship.

Fundamental to the disturbance in the back of the church is the
question: How can respect for the otherness of the other (Martin Buber)
be achieved if the other is regarded as the custodian and propagator of
falsehood? In different terms: Are there ways to deideologize† the Christian claim?

To return to the paradigm suggested at the close of chapter one, we
note that the move from chapter four to the present chapter reduces the
dominant and relevant variables from three (Jewish peopleness, Jewish
faith or Judaism, and Jewish Americanness) to two (Christian faith and
Christian Americanness). The reduction has two opposite kinds of
effect—a simplifying effect at the point of analysis, because laic considera-

---

*What is meant here is that Christian hostility to Judaism and Jews is the negative side and
consequence of the claim that Jesus is the Christ.
†A footnote of chapter two interprets "ideology" as primarily the propagating of ideas in the
service of collective self-interest. Deideologization is the struggle against ideology.

tions and problems are not decisive to Christian identity in and of itself; and a complicating effect of a substantive and existential sort, because any undermining of Christian faith must leave the Christian psyche forlorn. Many Jews see themselves as nonreligious yet appear to manage very well. But how can there be nonreligious Christians?

Because the morphology and the securities of laic identity are lacking to Christians *as Christians*, the Jewish-Christian encounter can become a more formidable threat to Christians than to Jews. In effect, the American Christian who is shorn of her or his faith becomes just an American. How could Americanness ever provide human beings with final spiritual meaning? And an ominous eventuality is implied here: May not one ultimate outcome of the dialogue prove to be an activating or reactivating of antisemitism?

The above state of affairs is congruent with the fact that in one respect, a highly significant yet almost unbelievable one, the Holocaust is a greater trauma for Christians than for Jews. For the moral credibility of Jewishness was never at stake in the *Shoah* (though the credibility of Jewish *faith* surely was). Once the moral credibility of the Christian faith is put in question, Christianness as such is threatened. Here is a major if below-conscious reason why, unlike the Jewish community, the Christian world has for the most part been unable to face up to the reality of the Holocaust. (Young, secularized, and nominal Christians, including many students, do not experience the same trauma that dedicated and knowledgeable Christians face, because these young people have thus far sought meaning for their existence—whether successfully or not—in ways beyond traditional faith. The sources of meaning in their lives are diffuse and pluralist. Their ignorance of traditional religious teachings—especially of the Christian "teaching of contempt" for Jews—is matched by their ignorance of the Holocaust. If ever the phrase "blissful ignorance" were psychologically and morally apropos, it is here.)

Today's Christian outlook respecting Christian-Jewish relations differs strikingly from the new Jewish stand respecting the world, Christians, and God. If the contemporary Jewish stance is noteworthy for its collective and individual self-affirmation combined with continued soul-searching, the Christian condition in the presence of Jews is such as to call self-affirmation into fundamental question, amidst soul-searching of a type radically different from the soul-searching of Jews. For the issue of moral credibility/noncredibility is the really salient challenge confronting Christians and their faith before the Jewish presence.

Much more is involved than a nagging awareness that Christian anti-semitism still abounds. For should the Christian faith finally be judged as morally noncredible, the Christian life itself would be shattered and the lives of Christians robbed of their spiritual and existential meaning. Here is another of history's ironies. In previous epochs the Jewish-Christian encounter entailed primarily a threat to Jews. In the *Shoah* Jewish survival was at stake amidst the surround of Christians and bystanders. But in the aftermath of the Holocaust, the moral question that is posed concerns Christian survival. In a sense, Christian children may be made to follow in the train of the Jewish children, though confronted not by physical extinction but by eventual spiritual death.

It is not the case that this issue of moral credibility has gained massive or even widespread attention within Christian circles. In truth, such concern remains relatively modest—a fact that itself sustains and compounds the Christian problem. Participants in the Jewish-Christian conversation differ in their assessments of the extent and influence of the changes that are taking place in the Christian church respecting the Jewish people and Judaism. For example, Monika Hellwig is considerably less negative than some other interpreters, probably including myself.[2] The discrepancies are not absolute nor is there a single definitive view. Each of us will make our own estimates of the number of pews that are, so to speak, occupied or affected by the demonstrators in the back of the church. I doubt that the most sanguine interpreter will adjudge (to quantify what is a qualitative issue) that more than one quarter of the available seats are filled by reformers and their knowing or unknowing supporters. The fact remains that those Christians who are dedicated to or directly involved in the enterprise of Christian-Jewish relations still find themselves having to expend consummate energy upon, and to pay unending attention to, the issue of Christian credibility.

A major abiding cause of this state of affairs is the character and content of the New Testament record as a continuing authority for the Christian church. The question of Christian moral credibility had its origin centuries before the Holocaust. It was created by the New Testament attitude to Judaism and the Jewish people, and it is perpetuated by that outlook. The complicitous and wrongful deportment of unnumbered Christians in the

Holocaust can hardly be received as the authoritative "moral" precedent for the church—at least not when human decency is a criterion. The all-decisive question is the moral and religious, and hence ontic, relationship between such deportment and an authoritative "Word of God," and hence between that kind of behavior and the nature and norms of Christian obligation. The Christian world may change, or seek to change. The New Testament does not change, and there is no way to change it. Christians who adhere to the final authority of the New Testament and/or of New Testament Christianity have been prompted to reject the mutual legitimacy of Judaism and Christianity, and they are quite "right," i.e., quite consistent. The New Testament provides a measure of support for mutual legitimacy and acceptance, but its prevailing thrust is one of Christian supersessionism. However, this condition does not stop some Christians from calling to witness elements within the New Testament itself in the struggle against that very supersessionism. Is there not as much ethical justification for contending that God works through minority witnesses as that God works through majorities? Indeed, as we think of such figures as the prophets, perhaps there is greater justification for a minority norm. Can there not be a prophetic rendering of the New Testament itself? David Tracy contends that "the heart of the New Testament message—the love who is God" ought to be able to "release the demythologizing power of its own prophetic meaning to rid the New Testament and Christianity once and for all" of the "anti-Judaic statements of the New Testament."[3] The New Testament scholar Raymond E. Brown advises that the anti-Jewish passages in the Gospel of John be retained as public readings, but only by following the readings with the preaching that the Johannine attitude is wrong for Christians today and must be rejected by them.[4]

Of additional relevance to the Christian condition in its independence of, though bond with, the Holocaust is the truth that the beginnings of a rethinking and reform of Christian faith and praxis respecting Judaism and the Jewish people were independent of or did not wait upon the Holocaust. John Haynes Holmes, Conrad Henry Moehlman, George Foote Moore, Reinhold Niebuhr, James Parkes, and Carl Hermann Voss are among the figures in point. Again, it was back in 1928 that the pioneer, major agency for Jewish-Christian understanding, the National Conference of Christians and Jews, was started (with, it is true, the combating of anti-Catholicism as a primary goal of the time). Jewish initiative lay to a large extent behind the interfaith movement. However, Protestants and Roman Catholics have always filled essential places in it. (Until now, the Eastern Orthodox churches have shown comparatively minor interest in Jewish-Christian relations. Anti-Israelism and anti-Zionism are by no means lacking in those churches.[5]) Furthermore, some Christian reformation, while initiated after 1933–1945, was motivated by influences other than the Holocaust as such, those influences extending to the concern to fight antisemitism in America. In this connection, we cannot forget that even if by some extraordinary miracle Christian behavior in the *Shoah* had been exemplary, Christian theological antisemitism would still have been regnant.

An additional consideration of fundamental moral importance is that most Christians living today had nothing to do with the Holocaust, and many of them are appalled by it. Where then would be the justification in holding such people blameworthy? Yet the issue of moral responsibility does enter in at one essential point: Do these people actively dissociate themselves from, and stand in judgment upon, the Christian teachings that had a part in bringing about the Holocaust? In different phrasing, what does it mean for a human being to continue to occupy a dedicated place in the Christian community? Ruth Kastning-Olmesdahl of the University of Duisburg (West Germany) comments upon the argument that those who took part in the Holocaust were no longer Christians: This is only a wrongful effort to release oneself "from the responsibility for a tradition of despising human beings."[6]

The United Methodist historian Franklin H. Littell brings together the Christian condition and the Christian challenge:

> Without centuries of antisemitic Christian preaching and teaching, Hitler could never have mobilized passionate Jew-haters and immobilized dispassionate spectators. In post-Holocaust Christian theology a radical conversion is required, a *metanoia* of spirit and mind in which nothing less than salvation is at stake. The timeless truths, called "principles" or "values" by liberal Protestants and "propositions" or "fundamentals" by conservative Protestants, belong to the pre-Holocaust era. The God who speaks—the God who acts—addresses specific persons facing specific choices in specific situations. In the Holocaust and its lessons God has put before Christians a choice between life and death, between salvation and damnation, as directly as long ago God confronted another people on Mount Carmel.[7]

The German Catholic theologian Johann Baptist Metz lays down a rule that makes vivid the link between Christian theological and moral reform and the question of Christian credibility: Stay away from a theology that could be the same before and after Auschwitz.[8] This is to say, any Christian theology of today that could have been formulated before or apart from the Holocaust is, in effect, pre-Holocaust theology even if composed after the Holocaust. To be denominated "post-Holocaust," a theology must range itself against the dominant characteristics of pre-Holocaust theology. Christians must ever be on guard against a theology that is not transformed by Auschwitz. We have just been suggesting that the history is not quite as simple as may be implied by this counsel. Nevertheless, Professor Metz is directing us to the radical, normative impact that the *Shoah* must have upon Christian faith and life. For it remains fatefully true that Christian reform did not manifest itself in very noticeable ways until after traditional Christian anti-Judaism and anti-semitism reached a culmination in the Holocaust. The fact that it took so evil an event for Christian thinking and behavior to begin to change is itself a judgment upon the Christian world. And in the measure that anti-Jewishness continues on, the Holocaust remains a contemporaneous event.

A final introductory point is that the new Christian reform is not going it alone, nor can it take all the credit for its advances. It receives substantial aid from America and from the Jewish community.

Just as peculiarly American norms and influences have greatly affected Jews and Judaism, so these elements have markedly conditioned Christians and the Christian church. Christianity in the United States has been long since transformed by the American values of democracy, religious pluralism, and tolerance, and in consequence has even been able, in turn, to help make those realities prosper.

On the matter of Jewish aid to Christian reform, the contribution from Jewish partners in the dialogue is immeasurable. And the impact of recent and current Jewish thought upon Christian thought cannot be overestimated. The more notable figures in North America include Emil L. Fackenheim, Irving Greenberg, Abraham Joshua Heschel, Alvin H. Rosenfeld, Richard Rubenstein, and Elie Wiesel. However, a great deal of the influence is a matter of the personal give-and-take and friendships that have developed among less noted people within the dialogue. This kind of thing often has greater impact at the grassroots level than do learned colloquia.

II

As we move into more specific issues, a word concerning methodology is once more desirable. Since, as has been observed, the Christian commotion remains at most a minority affair, it would be misleading to represent it as a dominating trend or achievement. Furthermore, the traditional Christian attitude concerning Judaism and the Jewish people is still very largely in force. When these two factors are put together it becomes clear that the new developments cannot be treated responsibly other than in the context of fundamental, ongoing conflicts within the church. This necessitates attention to continuing anti-Judaic and anti-Jewish elements in the Christian world as well as to recent and current efforts of an opposite persuasion and effect.

In chapter three I recorded, as a symbolic point of departure for the consideration of contemporary Jewish and Christian thinking and praxis, a watchword of Emil L. Fackenheim: "For Christians, the first priority may be theological self-understanding. For Jews, it is, and after Auschwitz must be, simple safety for their children." I suggested that Christian "theological self-understanding" be construed in ways that encompass "theological and moral self-criticism." This effort at theological and moral reform is developed in and through the four themes that follow and that comprise the main body of the present chapter. Internal Christian conflicts concerning Judaism and the Jewish people penetrate into many or most dimensions of Christian thought and life: God, authority, Christology, salvation, the meaning of Israel, the political order, anthropology, missions, etc. Our treatment has to be selective. Part III of this book will continue the discussion but with greater emphasis upon socio-political and practical aspects of the Jewish-Christian encounter. Since in the previous chapter the problematic of the Jewish mission and witness was treated last, I suggest we take up first the issue of the Christian mission and witness.

(a) Cross-purposes under the cross:
Christian mission and witness

Presupposed in our study is the view, widely accepted in Jewish and Christian quarters, that one cannot be a Jew and a Christian at the same time. Harold H. Ditmanson refers to this view as a basis for opposing the deceptions of such groups as "Jews for Jesus," which claim that through Christ the Messiah they have become "completed Jews." This claim at once misrepresents Christianity and flouts the integrity of Judaism.[9]

The honest alternatives for the Christian church are simple enough: either to engage in special efforts to enable Jews to convert to Christianity, or to refrain from doing so. But the question of the theological and moral justification/nonjustification of a mission to Jews is anything but simple.

It is said that the mission of the Jew has never been "to make the world Jewish but, rather, to make it more human."[10] In contrast, the church has sought to make the world Christian and—only?—in that way more human. Proponents of a missionary policy toward Jews proceed on the basis of both the persuasions we identified (chapter two, end of section two) as comprising the *fons et origo* of the Christian-Jewish conflict as a whole: the requirement to apply the Christian claim to Jews as Jews; and the duty to apply that claim to Jews as human beings. On the one hand, the Christian gospel is held to be the truthful fulfillment of Jewish faith and the only remedy for the wrongful Jewish rejection of Christ. And on the other hand, since the gospel applies to all humankind, no warrant is possible for excluding anyone from its blessings and saving power. Jews can hardly be made an exception. All human beings need the Good News. Missionaries to Jews have repeated unnumbered times that to bar Christian missionary endeavor to Jews would be a reprehensible case of antisemitism. What possible Christian or human justification could there be for keeping Jews out of the church? (One Jewish rejoinder here is that Christian conversionism actually sustains antisemitism since it reflects contempt for the Jewish faith-tradition and is hence one more act in "the history of malice."[11])

Carl F. H. Henry combines in a single declaration the two kinds of demands, upon Jews as Jews and upon them as human beings: "If one claims to know the truth about man's present felicity and final destiny and withholds it from his neighbor—whether gentile or Jew—he surely does not know the meaning of *agape*, or the import of truth."[12]

Those who are creating the commotion in the back of today's church are, for the most part, dissenters from Christian conversionism vis-à-vis Jews. Overall, the dissent rests upon both a prudential-historical base and an ontological-theological base, neither of which is entirely distinguishable from the other. According to the first emphasis, historical and moral experience is vital and indispensable to Christian decision-making. According to the second emphasis, the missionary decision must involve considerations of being and truth, not excluding the truth of God. In the latter respect, Carl F. H. Henry's reference to "the import of truth" is met on its own ground.

Robert E. Willis epitomizes a prudential-historical viewpoint:

> If, after Auschwitz, it is still possible for Christians to cling to the preten-
> sion that their story undergirds a responsibility for the conversion of Jews,
> then it is questionable whether we can learn anything from the events of
> history. For unless the consciences of those who profess to live out the
> Christian story can be reawakened by a consideration of these events—and
> the Holocaust in particular—then it would appear that there is a fatal
> quality to the outlook the Christian story engenders that prohibits signifi-
> cant revision. If that is the case, however, we are doomed to achieve not
> only an ambiguous, but a perverted and evil, embodiment of the deputy-
> ship entailed by that story.[13]

This plaint arises from the bond between the physical destruction of the Jewish people and a spiritual Final Solution (*eine geistliche Endlösung*), the Nazi program reincarnate at the religious level. It is held that, ultimately considered, there is no difference between murdering Jews in death camps and destroying their laic and spiritual identity through turning them into Christians.

In the present phase of the exposition the Jewish-Christian vis-à-vis is not being directly joined; we are reckoning with the Christian mission as an internal question of the church. However, it is widely felt today that outside judgments ought to be paid serious heed if the moral decisions of religious or other collectivities are to be responsible ones. This orienta-tion is adhered to on both sides in the Jewish-Christian dialogue. It is not inappropriate, therefore, to introduce a Jewish response to Christian conversionism, within a prudential-historical frame of reference: "Prior to the Holocaust, Jews could respect [Christian missionary] attempts, though of course considering them misguided. After the Holocaust, they can only view them as trying in one way what Hitler did in another."[14]

If it is to sustain itself, a prudential-historical outlook will eventually have recourse to ontological-theological criteria. There are at least two reasons for this (beyond, though grounded in, strictly epistemological reflection). For one thing, even after full attention is paid to historical experience, neither side in the Jewish-Christian confrontation is in a position to tell the other side what to believe or do. In this connection we note that the Holocaust has done nothing at all to annul the missionary stance toward Jews of Carl F. H. Henry and others. Henry has the human right to construct a wall around himself. Once behind the wall he has total immunity to any and all historical events, any and all human behavior, and any and all post–New Testament revelation. He writes that the answer to the question of Jesus as the Messiah of promise "is not settled by the fact that professing Christians have deplorably made the name of Christ a stumbling block among Jews, any more than the faithfulness of some ancient Hebrews [he must have meant to say faithlessness] invalidated prophetic religion by making Yahweh's name a reproach among Gentiles."[15]

Second, the obvious question arises of whether the Christian mission to Jews is to be restored in five hundred or a thousand years when the Holocaust will doubtless not marshall the moral force it has at present. Conceivably, in 3000 or 4000 C.E. the prudential-historical shoe may be on a different foot. But even as of 2000, Jews who become Christians are not sent to gas chambers. They remain living human beings, retaining all the joys and sorrows of the human condition. Any exact parallel between a physical *Endlösung* and a spiritual *Endlösung* thus gets into difficulties— *unless* a determining ontological-theological interdiction of the Christian missionizing of Jews is to be brought to bear. Belief in such a prohibition most often rests upon a categorical principle: It is wrong, objectively speaking and under *any* historical circumstance, to maintain that Judaism is to be abolished and that there are to be no Jews *as Jews*.

We are brought then to the ontological-theological level within an anti-missionary position. There are two sides to the coin: what is said about Christianity, and what is said about Judaism and Jewishness.

The Christian faith is held to be valid on its own terms. Down through the history of the church this persuasion has been expressed in infinite ways. One such expression of the singularity and integrity of Christianity is offered as the final theme of the present chapter (item d). Accordingly, it is not necessary to say more at this point except perhaps to recall the obvious consideration that in their lives and thought, Christians are continually "witnessing" to their faith in the presence of Jews and others, just as believing Jews witness to their faith.

The second side of the coin is the affirmation on the part of some

Christians that Judaism is perfectly valid as the faith of the Jewish people, also that Jews, whether or not religious, have a perfect right to exist as Jews. This point of view must be carefully distinguished from religious relativism and the abstract idea that one religion is as good as another. (We have to pass over the important question of the meaning and rationale of the church's mission or obligation to non-Jews.) Neither is the avowal of the truth of Judaism here being made from a Jewish standpoint or that of Christians who have become or desire to become Jews. The Jewish non-acceptance of Jesus is identified (on this Christian view) as faithfulness to the God of Israel in a world that remains unredeemed. The avowal of the truth of Judaism is deemed an objective necessity strictly from within a confession of the existential truth of Christianity. Christian conversionism toward Jews is considered a denial of God, through denying the unbroken covenant of God and Israel. The covenant between Israel and her saving God has been opened to Christians. Through the event of Jesus, Christians are grafted in to the people of God. Therefore, were the church to seek to convert Jews away from Judaism, it would be attacking not simply the Jewish community but the foundation of Christianity and hence Christianity itself. That would be a case of below-conscious recidivism into pagan origins, an act of self-destructiveness turned upon the "new man" or "new woman." It would be a Christian heresy.

In this latter context the asymmetrical aspect of the Jewish-Christian relation is once again exemplified. For possible objections among Jews to a Jewish conversionist effort toward Christians—and we have seen that such objections do get voiced—do not include the charge of self-destructiveness. We have earlier noted that the reality of Judaism and Jewishness is axiomatically independent of Christianity. Once all this is said, a most telling moral barrier nevertheless lies implicit within the avowal that the Christian faith has its foundation in Judaism. The difficulty arises out of the required differentiation—repeated again and again in this volume— between Jewishness and Judaism. A cardinal principle in the Jewish-Christian dialogue is that the act of self-definition is the exclusive reserve of each of the partners. Above, the expression is used, "the unbroken covenant between Israel and her saving God." The words may sound innocent enough. But to many nonreligious Jews, any such contention constitutes Christian imperialism (as it also indirectly helps, from that nonreligious point of view, to perpetuate Jewish wrongheadedness). Only

Jews have the right to define Jewish identity. We shall return to this most serious problem in Part IV of the book. For the present, the conclusion is reached that in contrast to the "theology of replacement" that suffuses Christian conversionism, we are now met with a Christian "theology of mutual recognition and co-existence," or with what has also been called "legitimate complementarity."[16]

To close our short treatment of the question of conversionism, an additional paradox within the Jewish-Christian relation may be discerned, a paradox nurtured by the external environment. In the world of today, Jewish and Christian views upon human salvation can alike cut in quite different directions. In a traditional *Jewish* frame of reference, the assumption that people do not have to be adherents of Judaism in order to gain wholeness or blessedness tends to militate against Jewish missionary endeavor. Yet the very fact that Judaism as a whole refuses to enter special soteriological claims for itself may have a certain appeal for some people and can actually serve to foster interest in Judaism and perhaps even conversion to that faith. In a traditional *Christian* frame of reference, to be convinced that people ought to accept the Christian faith in order to be saved or made truly blessed is clearly to underwrite Christian conversionism. Yet in contemporary society the absoluteness of this claim may have a way of prompting some people to have questions about Christianity, and may thereby inhibit a propagating of the traditional Christian mission. In both instances, though more in the Christian than the Jewish one, the voice of America is once again being heard.

(b) Cross-purposes under the cross: Christianity, Zionism, and the State of Israel

The conflict in the Christian world over a special mission to Jews is relatively mild in comparison to the internal Christian conflict respecting Israel. Overall Christian ambivalence to Zionism and the Jewish state reproduces the Christian ambivalence toward Judaism and Jewishness that we first noted in chapter two. The refusal or inability of some Christians to accept the State of Israel is a twentieth-century variation upon the traditional Christian denial of Jewish rights and integrity. The treatment of Israel as a nation very largely recapitulates the treatment of the Jewish people throughout Christian history.[17] Insofar as anti-Zionism and anti-Israelism reject the right of Jewish collective self-determination, while supporting other laic and national collectivities, they incarnate antisemitism. Today's massive support for Israel on the part of the people and government of the United States may tend to obscure the assiduous negativism respecting Israel that persists in the Christian world, particularly in ecclesiastic, bureaucratic, and journalistic circles. Anti-Zionism and anti-Israelism within and beyond the American Christian community have been of continuing influence, alongside a history of noteworthy and concerted Christian backing of Zionism and Israel.[18]

The Six-Day War of 1967 produced a serious crisis in Jewish-Christian relations due to widespread Christian failure to support Israel when annihilation was once more threatening the Jewish people.[19] This was devastating and disillusioning to Jews as well as to concerned Christians because of the widespread assumption that the non-Jewish world had learned from the Holocaust and was repentant for its earlier sins. The Yom Kippur War of 1973 renewed and exacerbated the crisis. Christian behavior, or inaction, under these threats served to compound traditional Jewish pessimism respecting the church's moral condition. It also angered and frustrated those Christians who were on the side of justice for Jews.

We are forced to remember that there was nothing new here. The reestablishing of the Jewish state was heavily opposed within the church, in liberal Protestantism as also in Catholicism,[20] not excluding the period immediately after the Holocaust. Of *The Christian Century* Martin E. Marty—its associate editor today—concedes that while during the Nazi era the editors strongly championed interfaith organizations and unwearyingly opposed American antisemitism, they were heavily conditioned by opposition to nationalism and by the influential endeavor to reduce Jewishness to a universal faith that would have "overcome" all its laic particularities. In consequence, *The Christian Century* was anti-Zionist. "The editors and most contributors did not support the State of Israel as created, or the way it was created. . . ." Only very reluctantly did *The Christian Century* finally "come to terms with the reality of Israel."[21] Nor has the atmosphere of non-support for Israel entirely disappeared from the pages of this most influential Protestant journal. In a final article of the *Century* centennial series at the close of 1984, the present editor surveyed the history of the publication between 1962 and 1971, analyzing its policy and contribution in relation to world-significant happenings of a moral, political, and religious nature. His analysis is totally silent upon the Six-Day War, and in place of reference to that momentous event there are singled out and reaffirmed as among the *Century's* "major concerns" the "rights of the Palestinians," by which are meant Palestinian Arabs, not Palestinian Jews.[22]

Christianity and Crisis, another influential American periodical, was most supportive of Israel while under the direction of Reinhold Niebuhr, a founder of the journal and a noted champion of Jewish rights. When Niebuhr's tenure ended, the journal came to develop an "evenhanded" or anti-Israel animus, to such a degree that Ursula Niebuhr, Niebuhr's widow, and their son Christopher insisted that Reinhold Niebuhr's name be removed from the masthead as a founding editor.[23] (For a third party to practice "evenhandedness," i.e., for it not to take sides, in the presence of a first party committed to the abolition of a second party is implicitly to throw in its lot with the first party. If it is genuinely to stand for the equal rights of the first and second parties—in this case, something that is rejected by the Arab enemies of Israel—a third party has no choice but to commit itself to the cause of the second party against the first party's effort at the other's destruction.)

When representatives of Vatican City are asked why that state has not afforded Israel diplomatic recognition the usual or "official" answer is that Vatican City does not recognize national entities that lack defined, internationally sanctioned borders. On that ground, Jordan as well lacks diplomatic recognition by Vatican City. However, even in Roman Catholic circles this answer is questioned. For example, Hans Küng identifies the answer as constituting "political opportunism and not fully suppressed anti-Jewish feelings."[24]

Conspicuous among detractors of Israel are Christian powers that be at the international and national levels: the World Council of Churches, the World Student Christian Federation (which denies outright Israel's right to exist), the National Council of Churches, and a number of denominational bodies.* The presence of strong anti-Israelism and antisemitism within these entities, in contrast to support of the Palestinian Arab cause, not excluding the PLO, is well known and has often been commented upon. Christian missionaries in the Arab world have done much to foment anti-Israelism in American church structures. Much of the problem centers in the moral question of whether an advocacy of "evenhandedness" is in fact evenhanded.

---

*The Quakers are particularly notorious for their anti-Israelism; see chap. 6.

In June 1981 at London-Colney, England, the Consultation on the Church and the Jewish People of the World Council of Churches—a group involving many veterans of Jewish-Christian dialogue and who are understanding of and sympathetic to Jewish concerns—recommended to the parent body a set of Guidelines for Jewish-Christian Dialogue. The recommendations contained a lengthy section identified by the phrase "The Land." By the time the Executive Committee of the WCC in Geneva had finished with the Guidelines and "commended" them to the churches (July 1982), the titled section on "The Land" had vanished completely. There remained but a few sentences referring to the State of Israel. The following was wholly excised: "Of particular significance [is] the understanding of the indissoluble bond between the Land of Israel and the Jewish people. . . . The need for the State of Israel to exist in security and peace is fundamental to Jewish consciousness and therefore is of paramount importance in any dialogue with Jews." Where the Consultation had expressed "the need of Palestinians for self-determination and expression of their national identity," the parent body substituted "the quest for statehood by Palestinians . . . as part of their search for survival as people in the Land . . . calls for full attention." Where the Consultation alluded to the special significance of the Land for Muslims and Christians, but stressed that "for Jews the relation to the Land is of an essential nature," the parent body contradicted this outright and insisted that the Land cannot be deemed more essential to one group than to another.[25] Thus, the work of the Consultation was thoroughly emasculated and left hardly recognizable.

The Dutch journalist J. A. Emerson Vermaat observes that the World Council of Churches has consistently refused to speak out upon the issue of oppressed Jews in Arab countries. When in 1975 the WCC General Secretary criticized the United Nations Assembly's identification of Zionism as a form of "racism and racial discrimination," the Fifth Assembly of the WCC meeting in Nairobi in November refused to support him. Instead, it arranged for a special book-stand for the PLO to distribute literature. The Sixth WCC Assembly in Vancouver in 1983 called for the establishing of a second Arab state in Palestine and a constituent place for the PLO in negotiations for "peace." The Assembly also charged that some Christians allow their guilt for the Holocaust to corrupt "their views of the conflict in the Middle East," in ways that entice them into "uncritical support" of Israeli policies. The WCC said nothing about the PLO reign of terror in Lebanon or the Syrian occupation of that land.[26]

Policy pronouncements of the National Council of Churches in the USA have taken positions comparable to the above. Over a recent short period of six years, this primarily liberal Protestant body managed to reject a resolution deploring the equating of Zionism with racism by the United Nations; to call upon the United States to establish contacts with the PLO; to demand of Israel that it include the PLO in peace negotiations; to call for a "settlement" along lines proposed by the PLO as "legitimate representative" of the Palestinian Arabs; to condemn Israeli responses to terrorist killings but to avoid condemning the terrorists; and even barely to favor the continuance of Israel as a Jewish state (by nine votes in a board of 250 members).[27]

The rationale of Christian anti-Israelism manifests both religious and extra-religious aspects. From an anti-Zionist point of view, the State of Israel incarnates characteristic Jewish effrontery. Did not "our Lord" prophesy doom upon an unbelieving Jerusalem, with the promise that "this people" is to be carried captive into all countries (Luke 21:5–6, 20–24)? The Jewish people's rejection of Christ dictates that they wander ceaselessly as pariahs amongst the nations. And since they have not (yet) turned from their sins and accepted Christ, their Zionist case lacks any legitimacy.[28] When Pope Pius X expressed to Theodor Herzl the Catholic Church's opposition to Zionism, he admonished him, "The Jews have not recognized our Lord, therefore we cannot recognize the Jewish people. . . . The Jewish faith was the foundation of our own, but it has been superseded by the teachings of Christ."[29] This Christocentric polemic still feeds conscious and below-conscious anti-Israelism in the church of today. (Strictly upon the pope's logic—or as a tour de force?—a possible mass Jewish conversion to Christianity would seem to legitimate a polity, or at least a homeland, for those Christian Jews. But would a world community of Christian Jews then have wanted to implement the Zionist goal? This appears highly unlikely, something that makes the pope's expressed logic preveniently gratuitous.)

On an extra-religious level, Christian anti-Israelism often takes the form of contending that the State of Israel is to be opposed because it has created untold suffering and injustice for Arabs. Thus, a group of Protestant missionaries and pastors (many of them Americans) serving at the time in Lebanon charged in an open letter that "the Zionists have driven the Arabs into the desert," that justice can probably be realized only "through armed struggle," and that Israel must be "dezionized," i.e., destroyed.[30]

In direct opposition to Christian anti-Israelism, the partisans of the commotion in the back of the church are highly supportive of Zionism and the State of Israel. Such Christian support goes far beyond the more or less condescending or grudging admission that Israel has a "right to exist." This reforming group answers Christian anti-Israelism through exposing a variety of influences contributing to that hostility: the impact upon Christians of Arab and pro-Arab propaganda; the church's persisting but erroneous retention (under the abiding conditioning of Hellenistic dualism) of a division between the "spiritual" and "material" domains, a division that is insupportable from a Jewish point of view;[31] the incapacity of many Christians to relate religious faith to the political order, or, more generally, to relate universal ideals to life's particularities; and the centuries-old forces of antisemitism and anti-Judaism.[32]

Positively construed, Christian Israelism, like Christian anti-Israelism, marshalls both religious and extra-religious arguments. The latter orientation (shared with many Jews) emphasizes empirical, human, and moral considerations: the integral right of the Jewish people to their own historic country, the simple justice of the matter. We have referred at various places to this foundation of the Jewish state. One further point may be included. Many extra-religious champions of Israel (though a number of religious ones as well) take exception to any religious pretension to what can be called "territorial fundamentalism," the assumption that the Jewish people possess the Land absolutely because of an absolute divine fiat. Such an assumption is cut from the same cloth as an absolutist religious denial of Israel's legitimacy. No human right can ever be construed as absolute.[33] But this is not at all to deny a constitutive link between the will and purposes of God and the Jewish state. Furthermore, opposition to territorial fundamentalism must not be allowed to sanction purely conditional Israeli rights, rights contingent upon special, exemplary moral behavior. In the theater of nation-states, no demands can be legitimately made of Israel that are not made of Egypt, the United States, India, Nigeria, Jordan, et al.

The religious orientation among pro-Israel Christian reformers emphasizes the link between the divine will and purpose and the Jewish state. Yet divergence quickly shows itself. In the one view God-and-Israel are assimilated to the Christian dispensation; in the contrary view it is the distinctive relation between God and the Jewish people that is retained. The former position is sometimes called "Christian Zionism," but the expression is misleading because the viewpoint is not genuinely Zionist, i.e., not genuinely supportive of Jewishness. An example of this outlook is the millennialist idea that God has returned the people of Israel to their Land in anticipation of the Parousia (Second Advent) of Jesus Christ. Jews are treated ideologically, i.e., as a means to a Christian end. There is nothing of Christian reformism in this ideology. Does it not violate the basic principle within the praxis of dialogue that the partner is to be received on his or her own terms? Christian reformers stress the contrary position listed: They firmly oppose the old ideology and practice of using Jews for Christian ends. These reformers maintain that Israel is a special event within the spiritual life of the Jewish people *and the Jewish people alone*. As James Parkes writes, the whole religious significance of the Hebrew Bible "ties it to the history of a single people and the geographical actuality of a single land."[34] On this position, the return of Israel to its Land can perhaps be read as an instance of the laughter of God (Ps. 2:4–6) at those who fabricated the horror tale of Jewish wandering because of the "rejection" of Christ.

Finally, a blending of religious and extra-religious elements is sometimes found. This is suggested in a speech of Pope John Paul II to a group of Jewish leaders in Mainz on November 17, 1980 (contrasting with the negative response of Pope Pius X to Theodor Herzl), "I look with you toward the destiny and the role of your people among the peoples. I gladly pray with you for the fullness of shalom for all your brethren of the same faith and the same people *and also for the land to which all Jews look with a special reverence*."[35] Again, there is the American network called the National Christian Leadership Conference for Israel, which came into being in 1978. An inclusivist grouping of mainline and evangelical Protestants and Catholics, blacks and whites, clergy and lay people, its motivations are prevailingly religious. But its program, conceived in a spirit of friendship and solidarity, extends to social and political action in the furtherance of Israel's security and wellbeing. Much of the work of the NCLCI is directed to Israeli-Arab peace. It is fitting, therefore, to include a word here in behalf of the cause and the rights of the Arabs of Palestine.

A lesson of the *Shoah* is that the political powerlessness of Jews made possible their destruction. This lesson is not without application respecting many of today's Palestinian Arabs. The parallel is not a complete one since these people as a whole already have a country, the sovereignty of Jordan, located in mandated Palestine and where the majority of the population are Palestinians. Nevertheless, hundreds of thousands of Palestinian Arabs outside Jordan are confronted by an uncertain fate.

Prerequisite to, though not a guarantee of, justice for them is an overall peace settlement in the Middle East. Yet at this writing, such a settlement seems extremely doubtful. And as Joan Peters shows in *From Time Immemorial*, the essence of the problem is the Arab world's effectual opposition to justice for the Palestinian Arabs as shown in the manipulation of these people as a weapon in the rejection of Israel.[36]

To bring together and conclude the theme of Christianity, Zionism, and the State of Israel: The problematic within the Christian outlook centers upon whether Israel (1) possesses any meaning or legitimacy at all; (2) embodies extra-Jewish meaning for Christians; or (3) lives exclusively upon the Jewish side in the Jewish-Christian encounter. Christian imperialism enters into (1) but is also a danger in (2). It is overcome in (3). For Israel remains the possession of the Jewish people* in exactly the way that the United States belongs to the American people. There is, lastly, the possible further complexity of Israel's meaning as perhaps transcending both the Jewish and the Christian worlds, as in a recent avowal that the State of Israel is an orienting reality for *all* post-Holocaust thought.[37]

The concern and support of many Christians for the State of Israel is for the sake of the wellbeing of Jews both as Jews and as human beings (antitheses of the two basic causes, it will be remembered, of the Christian-Jewish conflict as a whole). The Christian soul is here carried outside itself ("ecstasy" in its root meaning). This is of course not new. The history of collective and individual Christian charity *(agape)* toward humankind is one of the marvels of the world. We think, for example, of the story of selfless Catholic nuns across the years. But a peculiar and particularist note is sounded here, much like the special love of and for mother and father. In this discrete case, that kind of love—following upon long centuries of the children's prodigality (item [d] below)—is revealing its power for human reconciliation. Here is a sense in which Christians who step upon the soil of Israel have indeed returned home.† In a strange and radical way, one of the commandments is thus observed: "Honor your father and your mother."

---

*As this is written, approximately seventeen percent of the Israeli population are not Jews but Arabs, Druze, and others. All these people have full citizenship rights: they are Israelis. Yet it is so that Israel remains a Jewish state.
†Some 600,000 Christians come to Israel each year, slightly over half the number of all visitors.

(c) A Christological axis of Christian reform

On the Christian side, as reactively on the Jewish side, the issue of Christology is, theologically but also morally speaking, the heart of the Jewish-Christian encounter. From the back of the church Rosemary Ruether asks whether it is "possible to say 'Jesus is Messiah' without, implicitly or explicitly, saying at the same time 'and the Jews be damned.' "[38] How is Christian anti-Jewishness to be overcome unless there are revolutionary changes at the very heart of Christian teaching? The issue of Christian moral and religious credibility comes to focus in the issue of Christology. Emil L. Fackenheim argues that the link between Christian affirmation and Christian antisemitism is, after Auschwitz, *the* central question for Christian thought.[39] Langdon Gilkey, who is not intendedly anti-Jewish, recently wrote an introduction to Christian theology suffused with an anti-Judaism that is grounded in (proposedly) Jesus of Nazareth.[40] At base, Christian affirmation is Christological affirmation. Jewish spokespersons are reluctant, on moral grounds but also on prudential ones, to speak out for radical revisionism in Christian doctrine. They do not believe that it is right to interfere in another community's faith. And there is the persuasion among many Jews that, on balance, it is better (for Jews as for the world) that there be Christianity than that Christianity come to an end. However, a few Jewish thinkers argue in behalf of a rupture in "the traditional incarnational theology and its claims for Jesus as the promised Christ. This is to ask a great deal of Christianity," but for those of the persuasion of Richard L. Rubenstein, anything less is held to mean future tragedy and evil due to the perpetuating of Christian antisemitism.[41]

If the heart of the Jewish-Christian conflict is the issue of Christology, its inner heart is the affirmation/disaffirmation of the Resurrection of Jesus Christ—much more so than the Crucifixion. (Since the Resurrection is the inner heart of the Christian faith, there is no way to do Christian theology apart from the Christian-Jewish relation.) The essential link between the Jewish-Christian conflict and the Resurrection is brought out by setting in juxtaposition the views of three theologians, the American Catholic Rosemary Ruether, the French Catholic Jean Daniélou, and the German Protestant Jürgen Moltmann. In *Faith and Fratricide* as elsewhere Ruether maintains, with massive historical support and authentication, that the root of Christian antipathy to Jews and Judaism is the church's effort through its Christology to historicize eschatological reality, to bring the End-time into this world. The historical-theological legitimization of Christian supersessionism and triumphalism over Judaism and the Jewish people is a product of the continuously and contemporaneously asserted truth that in Jesus Christ the eschatological domain has entered into human history in definitive, salvational form. This testimony, it is alleged, is granted objective victory by God's act of Resurrection.

Jean Daniélou declares that the offense of the Jewish people is that "they do not believe in the risen Christ."[42] The distinctiveness of this charge is thrown into relief through the truth that in the nature of the case, other collectivities historically oppressed by the Christian world— blacks, women, the poor, et al.—could never be subjected to such an accusation. It is because of the special historical relation of Christians and Jews that the Resurrection comprises the center of the "theology of replacement," wherein the old, false Israel is reputedly superseded by the new, true Israel. A no less powerful and more concrete factor is the dogma that the event of the Resurrection is not a mere human idea or human spiritual experience but is exclusively a deed of God. It is God who, through a special sacred-historical act, vindicates the Christian faith in the face of its denial by the overwhelming majority of Jews. The insistence that the Resurrection is God's deed constitutes the foundation of Christian triumphalism and supersessionism. This brings us to Jürgen Moltmann.

In his authoritative work *The Trinity and the Kingdom* Moltmann declares that on the date of the Resurrection of the crucified Jesus, "the eschatological era begins." Moltmann is speaking of an actual, somatic Resurrection, with emphasis upon a genuinely divine transfiguration and transformation, and not a mere resurrection-idea or resurrection-ideal. For the teaching of the resurrection of the dead in the Hebrew Bible "already resists every form of spiritualizing reinterpretation." In the Resurrection, Jesus Christ "is exalted to be Lord of the dawning *kingdom* of God; and he is transfigured into the Lord of the coming *glory* of God. . . . God the Father glorifies Christ the Son through his Resurrection."[43] Here Moltmann is no more than describing the traditional, normative Christian position. But he is also witnessing to that position. (Elsewhere, Moltmann pleads for an anti-triumphalist version of Christian faith.[44])

The finding of Rosemary Ruether, who speaks from the rear of the

church, and the quoted attestations of Jean Daniélou and Jürgen Moltmann, who speak therein from the front of the church, are in diametric
conflict. Together the three point up the question of whether Christianity
any longer possesses moral credibility.

We are challenged by an all-decisive proposition: Once Ruether is held
to be correct that the Christian historicization of eschatological reality is
the foundation of Christian antisemitism, and once Moltmann is held to
be correct that the center and proof of the truth of Christianity is the
event of the Resurrection *as an eschatological event,* it follows that the
advocacy by Moltmann, a Christian theologian of the Germany of today,*
represents in clear and authoritative form the fateful, culpable union of
the Christian message and the murder camps, but contains as well the
Christian ideological contribution to a potential future Holocaust of the
Jewish people.

It is essential to bear in mind that the propositional truth here expressed does not, taken as a whole, involve, through either its structure
or its meaning, theological or moral differences of opinion. Accordingly, it
is not subject to purely theological or moral resolution. And it is not an
ideological statement. It is a logical-philosophic proposition, and ought to
be received as such. In consequence, the inexpugnability of its truth
could be offset only if one or another of its hypothetical constituents could
be justifiably removed. Such possibilities include a counteracting assertion that the Resurrection is not an eschatological event, and a denial that
the historicizing of eschatological reality in the Incarnation and Resurrection is in truth the root cause of, or even a factor in, antisemitism.
(Pinchas Lapide testifies to the Resurrection of Jesus as an actual happen-
ing—a highly exceptional position for a Jewish scholar—while denying
the Incarnation and the eschatological character of the event. All along
the line, Lapide stresses the Jewishness of the Resurrection. On the
Christian side, Carl E. Braaten rejects the view that Christology is the
root cause of Christian antisemitism.[45]) Yet the fact is that the proposition
as it now stands describes the logical and objective and hence inescapable
foundation of what Robert A. Everett identifies as the distinctive Christian ideology of Jewish victimization.[46] Each year at Eastertide, that

---

*The bond between Germany and the Holocaust is a truth of history; no *ad hominem* thrust
is intended here. Were *ad hominem* procedures at issue, my own German background
would also have to enter our purview.

ideology is granted special revitalization, but this takes place as well during the in-between times.

In view of the nature of our salient proposition, the conflict is seen to be open to philosophic treatment. Among the possible ways of meeting the impact of the proposition are the following. These choices are not wholly separable:

(i) A revisionist proposal that the foundation of Christian teaching be shifted from the supersessionism of Christology and Resurrection to something else. One example of this "something else" would be to concentrate in teaching and preaching upon the inclusion of Christians within the covenantal life of Israel.

(ii) A judgment that the Resurrection of Jesus Christ has not in fact occurred; positively put, an affirmation of that Resurrection as a still-future event. On this view the life of the church of today would be assigned a temporal-spatial locus, symbolically speaking, between Good Friday and Easter.

(iii) A proposal that the Resurrection of Jesus be retained as a divine event that has happened, together with a resolute endeavor to redeem it of its supersessionist and triumphalist connotations. This appears to be a delicate, hazardous, and formidable task yet it may be more realistic than the second alternative, which espouses, I think futilely, a frontal attack upon the Christian spiritual inheritance.

One possibility under (iii) is an effort to return the Resurrection to its home within the sacred history of Israel. This is exemplified in J. (Coos) Schoneveld, a Dutch Christian theologian who is General Secretary of the International Council of Christians and Jews. Schoneveld declares:

> The Resurrection means the vindication of Jesus as a Jew, as a person who was faithful to the Torah, as a martyr who participated in Jewish martyrdom for the sanctification of God's Name. What else can this mean than the validation of the Torah and vindication of the Jewish people as God's beloved people? The Resurrection of Jesus confirms God's promises as well as God's commandments to the Jewish people. . . . In the past, Christians have always connected the Jews with the death of Christ: they were called Christ killers, or the charge of deicide was thrown at them. I see the Jewish people in the light of the Resurrection. I see their survival throughout the centuries in the light of what the Resurrection means: the affirmation of the Torah, of the people of Israel, and of Jewish existence. Therefore, Christian affirmation of the Jewish people ought to belong to

the very center of the Christian faith. And if in the present the Jewish people gets a new chance to survive and revive, particularly through the State of Israel, I see this in the light of the Resurrection. . . .

It is not true that the church has replaced Israel or taken over its vocation. Both Israel and the church await the fulfillment of the Torah, when the image of God will be visible in the whole of humanity. The Jews await this final Day incorporated in the people of Israel, the Christians incorporated in the body of Christ. And both are judged by the same God to whom they have to answer, if they have been faithful to their particular vocation. The Jews have expressed their faithfulness in a "no" to Jesus as his church tried to take the Torah away from them. Christians may express their faithfulness in their "yes" to Jesus who embodied the Torah, and therefore also in a "yes" to his brothers and sisters, the Jewish people.[47]

Upon the reasoning of Schoneveld, the Resurrection is legitimately and morally restored to Christianity, because the poison of victimization has been drained away from it.

In whimsical variation upon this third view, one could fabricate a decision of God to demonstrate that he/she was on the side of the Pharisees against the Sadducees in the conflict over whether the dead are resurrected. In order to make clear that he/she was dead serious on this matter, God raised his/her Pharisee son Jesus from the dead. In the Resurrection we may thus hear a further echo of the laughter of God.* But John T. Pawlikowski points to a complication: "The Pharisees insisted, in keeping with their community orientation, that no individual would arise until the Messianic Age since no one could enjoy full salvation until the community has reached its total development."[48] This suggests that in order to stay with the divine whimsy one would have to add that God was now getting a jump on his/her Pharisee friends.

In the above three alternatives—others may be suggested—necessary allowance is made, at least implicitly, for the philosophic-logical inexorability of the Ruether-plus-Moltmann proposition. However, the proposition is also being responded to in theological, moral, and de-ideologizing ways. Whether one or another of the three responses is either convincing or feasible is another question, and a highly controversial one. In any event, the proposition has the function of reminding us that a most important moral challenge to the post-Holocaust church

---

*According to the biblical record, Jesus was not the first or only human being to be raised from the dead; see I Kings 17:22; II Kings 4:35; 13:21; and cf. Matt. 27:52–53; John 11:1–44.

is the relation between a "theology of replacement" and the Resurrection of Jesus, and thus between the Holocaust and the Resurrection. Fresh and venturesome thinking on this subject is barely getting under way.

(d) Christian singularity, Christian integrity

I referred in section one of the present chapter to the issue of Christian moral credibility in the aftermath of the Holocaust. The issue surfaced again in the section just concluded. May such a state of affairs have the effect of calling into question the integrity of the Christian faith itself? We have alluded more than once to the moral asymmetry within the Jewish-Christian relation. And—it could be added—even if reformers and other penitents such as those noted in this chapter have started a small disturbance, what of the historic and contemporary Christian community as a whole, particularly in its structures of social power and its religious psychology of self-satisfaction? Most serious of all, the Christian dogma of a triumphalist Resurrection that is conducive to a victimizing of Jews continues to stand at the center of the church's teaching and preaching.

A poignant eventuality suggests itself: the forlornness of today's Christian. Are Christians left utterly ashamed, utterly bereft, utterly alone? Is that the lesson of the *Shoah* for the Christian world? Have Christians betrayed their own human dignity? Are they destroyed, in a spiritual and moral sense, under the relentless blows of an unanswerable moral assault upon their faith?

One way to speak for Christians and their faith in the shadow of the *Shoah* and amidst the persisting presence of anti-Judaism and antisemitism is along the following line:* These human beings are indeed forlorn, yet they are not forlorn. They are to be ashamed yet not ashamed. They are bereft yet not bereft, alone yet not alone. As the Letter to the Ephesians describes the matter—transcending any special historical situation yet applying to every situation—the Christian, the pagan outsider, the one who is "alienated from the commonwealth of Israel," the stranger "to the covenants, having no hope and without God in the world" (2:12), is nonetheless, through the history of the Jew Jesus, granted acceptance. To be a Jew, traditionally speaking, is to be accepted of God

---

*Once again a shift occurs here to religious language, if only for the sake of the point of view being represented.

in and through the community of Israel (whether or not one believes in God). To become a Christian is to be accepted of God beyond yet in some way through the community of Israel (and by virtue of a special trust in the God of Israel). In her memoir upon the life and work of James Parkes, Rose G. Lewis refers to a crucial sense in which "Christianity does not begin with Jesus, who was in any case a faithful Jew. It is rooted in Judaism, and the Covenant at Sinai is the deepest root of all and the primary source of comfort and legitimacy."[49] The Christian faith is nevertheless tied to and indeed made possible only by the history of Jesus. What this means, and what therefore the confessed events of Incarnation-Crucifixion-Resurrection are to mean, is today receiving serious attention. Once the claim is made that God acted to bring non-Jews into the family of Israel, the affirmation/disaffirmation and interpretation of these exact events, while very important, is not of final importance. We are advised that "the wrath of men shall praise" God (Ps. 76:10). The same conviction may be applied to human errors and limitations of various sorts—not excluding the error of the small number of first-century Jews who, against Judaism, saw in Jesus the Messiah and Redeemer.

Yet Christianity retains its own integrity. It is not to be reduced to a version of Judaism,* however surely it rests upon the rock of the God of Judaism—the graceful God who yearns for and establishes righteousness, the God who loves, the God who weeps. Christians fall amongst those who have betrayed the originative people of God. Christians are nobodies who are condemned for, among other sins, the satanic praxis of antisemitism. But they are also received by a voice that says "I accept you."

The Christian is the prodigal son, the prodigal daughter, the prodigal child. In Jesus' story the decision of the younger son to turn back to his father's house involved a trick. The prodigal was without food, and all he wanted really was something to eat. So he hit upon a stratagem. Upon his arrival home he would say, "Father, I have sinned. . . . I am no longer fit to be called your son." Yet the deceit was immediately made gratuitous. He was accepted, tricks and all. Before hearing a single word, his "father ran to meet him, flung his arms round him, and kissed him. . . . The father said to his servants, 'Quick! fetch a robe, my best one, and put it on

---

*Nor is it to be reduced to an exclusively gentile reality, after the fashion of one or more contemporary theologians. Such rigidity is unconsciously or consciously prejudicial toward Jews.

him; put a ring on his finger and shoes on his feet. Bring the fatted calf and kill it, and let us have a feast to celebrate the day.' " To what purpose? It was not that the son had all at once overcome his prodigality and was now getting rewarded as a changed human being. That is not the point of the merrymaking or of the story, and it is not the point of the Christian gospel. The feast could only be held because the father had learned that his son was alive: " 'For this son of mine was dead and has come back to life; he was lost and is found.' And the festivities began" (Luke 15:18–24, NEB). Grace is the act of accepting the unacceptable. Where sin abounds, grace abounds the more. Grace says: "You are accepted."[50]

The existential power in the tale of the prodigal is consonant with the fact that it is wholly within the church, if only in its rear sections, that the hubbub we have chronicled has developed—not somewhere out on the streets or far away. Most of these reforming Christians intend to keep on being Christians.

Insofar as Christians are accepted by grace (together with Jews[51]), they can enter the dialogue as equals—however evil their past and their present, however disreputable and torn the baggage they must carry to the meeting, and however grievous their peculiarly Christian idolatries. Christianity in its *sine qua non* is not cast away.

Christians are people who have been imputed a dignity equal to that of Jews. A Jewish-Christian relationship becomes a possibility, and hence a Jewish-Christian dialogue can begin as part of that relation. The imputation of equal dignity is strictly that; there is nothing here of achieved goodness. As a matter of fact, a case can be made that any claim (not only Christian but also Jewish) to a consummated goodness will end up fostering evil. Irving Greenberg interprets as follows part of the contribution of Elie Wiesel: Moral viewpoints that consider themselves adequate thereby become "the enemies of what they think they stand for. Christians who feel that the crucifixion sacrifice of Jesus satisfactorily overcomes evil become collaborators in indifference and continuation of the evil," just as "Jews who insist that God fully redeems and punishes go beyond the criminals of genocide in adding, on top of their unjustified suffering, cruel judgment against the innocent victims. . . . Faith must be taught with full inclusion of the reality of doubt and evil."[52] Were the Christian affirmation of human acceptance allowed to rest upon the claim of a human achievement of goodness, rather than upon a divine Yes to human beings who in truth remain unacceptable, the consequence would be evil. Any pretension to human goodness for Christians would only perpetuate the supersessionism and imperialism that mean anti-Jewishness. The one way out of the prison is an anti-perfectionist concentration upon the divine acceptance. However, that concentration cannot be permitted to sanction irresponsibility. Do we not have at this point a special reminder and gift from the Jewish community to the Christian community? (Otherwise, Christians would be tempted by the demonic condition of the missionary who claimed that a last-minute conversion to Christianity would save Adolf Eichmann's soul but that the souls of Eichmann's victims were not saved.[53] Only one claim is more questionable than the insistence that anyone is absolutely unredeemable: an insistence that anyone is absolutely redeemable.)

The special summons to Christians remains in force: to transform the small commotion in the back of the church into a great chorus that will shake the foundations. In that way these Christians will be allying themselves with the future (Isa. 24:18). And they will be meeting the Christian imperative cited near the end of chapter two, "We love, because he first loved us" (I John 4:19). In response and gratitude to the love of God, Christians love other people. The Christian life—like the Jewish life—embodies an age-old dialectic, that of divine grace in tension with human obligation: "Work out your salvation in fear and trembling; for God is at work in you, inspiring both the will and the deed, for God's chosen purpose" (Phil. 2:12).

However, the above summons to Christian responsibility does not meet or resolve a most grave, objective moral problem: On the one hand, the Christian is said to be "accepted." Yet, on the other hand, the church's teaching of an imperializing and victimizing Resurrection continues on. How is it possible to reconcile human acceptance and human criminality? We shall hold this question for our last chapter. But we cannot here omit a fundamental challenge to Jewish thinking today: how to relate Judaism's God of history to the patent truth that non-Jews have been accepted by that God. This means that in the very name of the one and only God of Israel, Christianity has to be taken with much greater seriousness than is reflected in the mere concession that Judaism does not pass judgment upon other faiths, or in the highly generalized affirmation of the Noachian laws and covenant. Is not Jewish theology obliged to work out a positive position upon the unique role and particularity of Christianity today?

Finally, to restate the ontology of human acceptation along lines that fit into the relative-dialogic Jewish-Christian encounter now taking place within a post-*Shoah* world: Modern Jews, particularly in America, have tended to celebrate the goodness of humankind (in the very face of historic Jewish victimization by human sin), and in consequence the depravities of the Holocaust could just about prostrate them.[54] By contrast, the Christian church has tended more to sustain the truth of the evil of humankind (in the very face of all the church's own blessings and power in the Western world), yet it is the sinfulness (idolatry) of Christians themselves that has helped them ignore the Holocaust, just as this sinfulness once made possible that very event. Thus are Jews and Christians brought together and addressed by a single and singular question: How are you going to think and act responsibly in the presence of human sin[55] but as beings who are nevertheless made in the image of God, the God who judges you and yet, weeping, accepts you nonetheless? "I will not execute my fierce anger" (Hos. 11:9). "You shall say to them this word: 'Let my eyes run down with tears night and day, and let them not cease' " (Jer. 14:17).

PART III

◆

Where the Action Is

6

◆

Irons in the Public Fire

Having reckoned in Parts I and II with the foundations and lineaments of today's Jewish-Christian meeting, we take up in this chapter and the next a few highly practical and controversial issues and developments in the public moral order.

I

Several orienting comments are appropriate.

(a) The American Jewish community manifests a large measure of agreement upon antisemitism, attempted Christian conversion of Jews, the State of Israel, and attitudes respecting Jewish-Christian relations. While Christian consensus upon these issues has been growing, it does not compare to the Jewish consensus.

(b) When we turn to other issues, variety increases and abounds. And this is so, in differing degrees, upon both sides of the arena. As pointed out in chapter one, some Jews at times range themselves with Christians against other Jews, and some Christians at times range themselves with Jews against other Christians. With the contemporary women's movement in mind, the most obvious and yet most striking new alignment within the dialogue, at least potentially, is Christian and Jewish females vis-à-vis Christian and Jewish males (chap. 7).

(c) It is sometimes necessary, in contrast to the exposition prevailing to this point, to subdivide the general categories of Jews-Judaism and Christians-Christianity. Within the subdivisions conflict often is found. Robert A. Handy reminds us that the threefold distinction Catholic-Jewish-Protestant distorts the overall American religious picture, which is in fact "Catholic-Jewish-Orthodox [Christian]-Protestant-Mormon-Pentecostalist-New Thought-Humanist," together with numerous other groupings and many further subgroups within those here identified.[1] It can be maintained, nonetheless, that "Catholic," "Jewish," and "Protestant" remain meaningful and identifiable categories in American society, and are open to useful study and analysis.

Many times, conservative Catholics, Orthodox Jews, and fundamentalist Protestants have more in common, religiously and morally speaking, than they have with their respective liberal opposite numbers.[2] And from the shared point of view of liberal Catholics, Jews, and Protestants, the contrasting conservative positions are in each case objectionable.

American Judaism and American Protestantism are notably democratic religious phenomena, in contrast to Catholicism, with its markedly authoritarian religious structures. On specific issues of interpreting *halakhah*, majority rabbinic vote has always ruled. Many Protestant denominations maintain local congregational autonomy. It is true that since Vatican Council II, democratic elements have become much more evident in the Catholic Church, with special reference to the stress upon religious freedom, the positive role of the laity, and greater decentralization along national lines.[3] However, one Catholic spokesperson is very skeptical that a new consensus theology is realizable in the Catholic Church, so long as "the guardians of the ecclesiastic hierarchy" are able to keep their power.[4]

We have noted that for the "civil Judaism" of America, individual conscience is a prevailing arbiter of religious belief and practice. The same applies, in varying measures, within American Christianity. True, in Protestant fundamentalism the letter of Scripture is a powerful competitor to conscience and often gains the victory. In some fundamentalist institutions a tenured professor found equivocating on biblical inerrancy could very well be dismissed from his or her post. In Catholicism church authority plays a comparable role, and in the same way often emerges the victor over conscience. These restrictive elements find a certain counterpart, but usually a less fateful one, in authoritative claims for *halakhah* within the Jewish community. Notwithstanding such complications, the American religious ethos as a whole proclaims the supremacy of conscience. To the degree that this ideal is able to break through, the Jewish-Christian dialogue becomes a celebration of human freedom.

An intriguing dimension of the Jewish-Christian encounter is the way the participants shift places and alliances as there are shifts in the concrete issues at hand. Thus, in the matters of clerical celibacy, divorce, and abortion Catholicism stands on the one side and—*mutatis mutandis*—

Judaism and Protestantism stand on the other. But on the power and authority of tradition, Jews and Catholics are much closer than either party is to Protestants. Along a not wholly dissimilar line, a communitarian ethic is dominant within the Jewish and Catholic communities, in some contrast to a still-persisting Protestant individualism. On the other hand, Catholics and Protestants observe sacraments while Jews do not (in the sense understood by Christians). Yet here too things are not so simple. Marriage is a sacrament for Catholics (cf. the prohibition of divorce) but it is not a sacrament for Protestants. Further, the authority of tradition applies to Orthodox Jews more than to many other Jews. And so it goes. . . .

For the most part, we are not able to pursue the many variations of belief and practice found inside the Christian community and inside the Jewish community. Yet sometimes such discrepancies cannot go unnoticed. For instance, on the Christian side identifiable differences are to be noted between liberal Protestants and evangelical Protestants upon the subject of attitudes toward Jews. One recent study found that liberals scored relatively low on antisemitism and relatively high on antagonism to Israel, while evangelicals scored relatively high on antisemitism and also relatively high on support for Israel.[5] Tom F. Driver writes, "There is little room for doubt that right-wing evangelical Christianity in this country is deeply anti-Semitic. It is also true that this group is pro-Israel. We are thus presented with a great and frightening irony. The most pro-Israel group in American Christianity is also the most anti-Semitic." However, as Driver continues, this cannot obscure the truth that liberal Christianity tends to be soft on antisemitism.[6]

(d) Widespread disparities are sometimes found between institutional norms and teachings and the praxis of the people. For example, most American Catholic couples do not honor the Church's prohibition of artificial birth control. Some eight million Catholics are divorced. According to many surveys and polls, most American Catholics reject their Church's absolute prohibition of abortion. Of the 1.5 million American women who undergo abortions each year, about one quarter are Catholic. Recently, I saw on television an American Catholic woman identified as of Polish descent who, when apprised of a certain cardinal's stricture upon abortion, responded with a Bronx cheer. That her own national background coincides with that of the present pope proved, in that context, to be non-inhibiting. Again, while there is marked unity among Jewish authorities against mixed marriage, because of its being a threat to Jewish laic survival, the rate of marriage with non-Jews is, as earlier noted, very high. (Is it any longer possible in our world to implement an ideal morality through religious authority—or, for that matter, through political authority? The Bronx cheer, audible or silent, seems to have become endemic—and well beyond the Bronx.)

(e) In keeping with the absence of any inherently laic component within Christianity, and also with the church's proclivity for spiritualization, the Christian world has sometimes been tempted away from a positive theology of the secular (political-legal) order, even though that area is constituent to any overall theology of the created world. A consequence is a partial failure to make connections with the moral realm in all its concreteness. This condition is found much more in Protestant than in Catholic Christianity. In theory, the Jewish stress upon the goodness of creation, upon the celebration of this life, and upon a practical ethic for a specific people helps prevent such a state of affairs. Yet the Jewish contribution has itself been impeded. For only within recent years has the Jewish community gained the opportunity to implement without limitation an integral Jewish theology of politics, not just for Jews but for the world at large. Much work needs to be done here. Furthermore, the relatively greater stress within the Christian community upon the sinfulness of humankind has helped keep alive for the church a transcending judgment upon the idolatries of social and political systems, claims, and achievements. The more that Christians are liberated from triumphalism, the more are they set free for moral and political responsibility. The more Jews are liberated from powerlessness, the more are they set free for creative political and social action in the world.

(f) A reminder is apropos respecting the minority-majority relation of Jews and Christians in America, first referred to in chapter one. Jewish involvement in the social and political order just cannot afford to lose sight of the minority condition of the Jewish community. This helps to orient Jewish positions upon such issues as religion-state relations and intermarriage. Where acculturation and social integration are regnant, intermarriage will thrive. Yet, as we have emphasized, it is within a free society that American Jews live as a minority. The integrity of religious and ethnic groupings is basic to the American ideal. Here as at many places people are enabled to pay their money and take their choice—

though the statement of this opportunity is only an ironic metaphor when it comes to the millions of Americans who remain below the poverty line.

(g) When Jews and Christians meet in conclave the public pronouncements they make upon religious or social issues will, expectably, tend toward conservatism. Moderation is a bare stone's throw from status quoism. More radical members of the two groups (to the right or to the left) may well join forces upon ideas or policies of a more revolutionary sort. But one could hardly identify such radicalness as typifying the Jewish-Christian relation or achievement as such. One value in reporting upon the points of view of individual Jewish and Christian figures is that they often charm us, blessedly, along the leading edges of contemporary thinking, freeing us from the stodginess of compromise.

II

There follow brief critical commentaries upon just three vital contemporary issues that, beyond the largely theological-historical themes earlier surveyed, go to supply the agenda for many a real-life Jewish-Christian encounter of today. I do not pretend to a complete or balanced, comparative intergroup and interfaith representation. The substantive and judgmental materials to come, together with my own critical remarks, are offered primarily with heuristic purposes in view. The intent is to stimulate thinking, foster argument, induce reflection, encourage research. Accordingly, the method is to a considerable extent impressionistic. Within each topic, there is rampant picking and choosing. The issues chosen comprise only a few of infinite possibilities. Yet these subjects are among those that are generating much discussion and controversy, not alone between the two communities but inside each of them.

(a) Religious liberty, religious tyranny, and the state

Here is a little potpourri: The American Coalition for Traditional Values contends that since "Bible-believing Christians" represent a minimum of twenty-five percent of the work force, they ought to be given that proportion of civil service positions. The ACTV operates a "talent bank" to get "true Christians" into "positions of authority in government." A *Business Week*/Louis Harris poll finds (September 1984) that by a margin of 71–26 percent American voters maintain that a minister ought not endorse political candidates because of their reflection of church policy on abortion and school prayer. The Southern Baptist Convention, traditionally composed of staunch advocates of religion-state separation, nevertheless votes to endorse the U.S. president's call for a constitutional amendment authorizing nonsectarian prayer in the public schools. The National Jewish Community Relations Advisory Council (which, according to Balfour Brickner, is "possibly the most broadly representative consortium in American Jewish life") states that legislation permitting or requiring prayer in public schools is unconstitutional and unwise public policy. The Union of Orthodox Jewish Congregations of America does not object to provision for silent meditation in public schools. A president of the United States calls for a constitutional amendment to forbid abortion. A leader in the National Association of Evangelicals (founded 1942) estimates that the evangelical community today supports candidates for office who are anti-abortion in an approximate percentage of 75–25. An Episcopal bishop contends that the issue of abortion ought "not be dictated by government, whether it is in the courts, the executive or the legislative arm." One influential American rabbi declares that an anti-abortion amendment would induce civil disobedience amongst those Jews who live in accordance with *halakhah*, because *halakhah* enjoins abortion in certain limited cases. Some Orthodox Jewish leaders go against a previously unified Jewish position by opting for state support of parochial (religious) schools. A Catholic ethicist uncovers a "blueprint for a fascist family" in the relevant policies of the radical fundamentalist right. A representative of the Rabbinical Council of America (Orthodox) points out that "the separation of church and state is a political, not a religious principle. Indeed, within Judaism itself, the political and the religious are inseparable; the city of man is incorporated into the city of God." The Executive Committee of the Union of American Hebrew Congregations (Reform) "expresses profound concern over the grave erosion of the commitment of all branches of government to the constitutional principle of separation of church and state." And a sociologist asks, "How can one hold that there is a relationship [among religion, politics, and morality] when it comes to matters of school prayer and abortion, but not when it comes to matters of poverty, civil rights, and the prevention of nuclear war?"[7]

Such vignettes as these raise in all its complexity and poignancy the question of religion and the state. (The phrasing "church-state relations" is customarily employed, even among Jewish spokespersons. In the present commentary "religion-state" is substituted because of the Christian connotation of "church.")

Many of the religion-state issues of today are carryovers of the Protestant era of American history. These include tax exemption of the property of religious institutions, prayer and Bible reading in the schools, religious displays on public property, the assessing of political candidates on the basis of religious affiliation, and legislation relating to birth control.[8]

If the Christian people of early America could see themselves as delivered from European church oppression, the Jewish people of America retain comparable and more recent collective memories. Significantly, the experience of the Christians itself helped create political instrumentalities for ensuring the protection of Jews and others from the very Christians who, though having fled from church and government oppression, were themselves not exactly bursting with toleration. Having lived for centuries under a hostile Christendom, Jews are particularly sensitive to the need for socio-political instruments to keep religious imperialism from translating itself into public policy. Yet here American Jews speak not alone for themselves but, implicitly, for the wellbeing of the nation as a whole.

Jews are sometimes accused of defending a "godless" public school system. Many people fail to appreciate what the public educational system has meant for Jews: "It was America itself, the land of equality, the happy home of persecuted minorities, where children were free to be themselves without fear of the lurking authority of church or parson!"[9] If the latter fear has not had a comparable place in the lives of Christian children, the public educational system has nevertheless benefited all Americans.

Two major and closely related social ends of the American system may be singled out: public order and peace, and liberty for religion. The first of these is given voice by Henry Steele Commager: "We do not limit prayer in public schools or forbid religious 'tests' because the Constitution so provides; the Constitution so provides because experience taught its

Framers that such actions would menace the peace and harmony of our society."[10] On the question of school prayer, I seem to remember that while at school, children spend good amounts of time in prayer, usually of a silent but intense kind: "This is the worst test she ever gave us. Dear God: Please help me pass it." "He is looking straight at me! Dear God: Make him ask someone else that question." "There goes the most gorgeous creature I ever saw. Dear God: Help her to notice me." Accordingly, it proves to be an enormous, probably impossible task, despite the fears of many, to "take God out of the schools." Why is it that those who voice the fear that the opposite is the case are most often either running for political office or are religionists of identifiable stripes? (In 1984 the National Association of Evangelicals endorsed the U.S. president's effort to amend the Constitution to provide prayer in the public schools. The Jewish community as a whole opposes the prayer amendment.[11])

The second purpose of the American system was early expressed by James Madison: "The Constitution does not create a shadow of right in the general Government to intermeddle with religion." In other words, the freedom of religion is to be protected at all costs. There is no question of affording Americanism or so-called secular humanism or peculiarly worldly idolatries a pretext to rule over religious faith. The American system is involved in preventing those very consequences. The American arrangement entails secularity and neutrality, not because of any opposition to religiousness but for just the opposite reason: to guarantee the free exercise of faith. A primary instrument of this guarantee is to prevent any one religious party or religio-political entity from preempting religiousness. Safeguards for religious liberty are as beneficial to the Christian majority as to the Jewish minority and other religious minorities. Thus, no Christian grouping has profited more from the American system than American Catholicism, now by far the largest single Christian community in the United States. However, threats to the ethos of religious and social pluralism, and to religion-state separation, continue to arise. They largely come from Christian sources. Here is an added mark of asymmetry within the Jewish-Christian relationship.

There is a fundamental disparity between the notion of a "Christian America" and a life for free Christians and others in a pluralist America. Proponents of the former idea operate under the assumption that America is not only a Christian nation but a Christian nation on their terms. These people do not in actuality mean to have an America free for *all* Christians (or others). "Christian" means Christian strictly in the way these devotees understand it. Their tacit anti-Jewishness is matched by their tacit opposition to Catholicism, to liberal Protestantism, and indeed even to conservative forms of Christianity other than their own. The brands of fundamentalism are as conflictive as they are legion. In truth, the United States is not a Christian country in any official political or national sense. It carries in its Constitution various built-in safeguards against Christian or other religious tyranny. (In this respect, it retains a partial advantage over Canada. On the other hand, Canada has been especially sensitive to Jewish laic rights.[12]) It is sobering to remember that one modern nation to designate itself constitutionally a "Christian nation" is the Republic of South Africa.

Protestants (and others) who seek "to defend viewpoints and practices that once may have been understandable but are now outmoded" only handicap themselves from "serving the present and facing the future."[13] However, the newer socio-religious picture is complicated by resurgent forms of Christianity, especially the one identified as "evangelical." Increasing numbers of these advocates reject out of hand the claim that their viewpoints and practices are "now outmoded."[14] They identify their beliefs and behavior as loyalty to the "truth." This trend is naturally conducive to opposition and even alarm among Jews as among many Christians.

For all its innocent-sounding name, the American Coalition for Traditional Values is constituted of the radical Christian right. In his writings Tim LaHaye, chairman of ACTV, stresses that the Jews rejected the Son of God and "brought the judgment of God upon themselves and their land." He identifies Catholicism as a "false religion." He again and again laments the (reputedly) sinister designs of 275,000 "secular humanists" who "run" the government, the media, and the public schools.[15] The ACTV program potentiates a Jewish-Christian confrontation, with special reference to the Jewish community's commitment to the separation of religion and state. Yet as well the ACTV program joins the issue between the radical Christian right and countless other Christians who are equally devoted with Jews to the American system. Baptists are noteworthy here. Most Jews and many Christians are thus made allies against a group of Christians in defending the American tradition and pledging themselves to its perpetuation. (Millions of evangelical Christians in the United

States do not advocate breaching the wall of separation between religion and state.)

The exercise of religious freedom is hardly immune to the afflictive praxis of human sin. We need only think of the religious schools that were recently created as a device to forestall racial integration and that try to plead innocence of racism by hiding under the cloak of religious liberty. The American system is a paradoxical tribute to, at one and the same time, the religious dimension of life and the need for constraints upon that dimension when it tries to play God and becomes tyrannical. In this country, intolerance at the religious level is comprehended, tacitly, as a form of social sin that must be controlled. Furthermore, the peculiarly American achievements against intolerance and religious tyranny may themselves be interpreted religiously and theologically, as pointing to the judgment of God upon the idolatries and sin of the very parties who claim to be espousing the truth of God.[16]

Religious pluralism, religious freedom, and political democracy thus combine as, at once, singular protectors of religion and guardians against the peculiar sins that live off religion.

(b) Are the "peacemakers" perforce blessed?

The perennial questions beset us of war and peace, violence and nonviolence, aggression and responses to aggression.

Judaism has always been resolute against any dualism that makes the realm of the spirit alone good and treats the world of matter and physical force as inherently evil. The acknowledgment that the world is unredeemed helps to inhibit political perfectionism within the Jewish ethos. By contrast, the Christian stress upon redeemedness has a way of nurturing such perfectionism. Yet since Christian societies and nations have been anything but distinguished for their pacifism, the problem must lie at a deeper level than can be comprehended through attention to differing teachings upon redemption. If pacifism has never in fact been the dominating policy within Christianity (with due allowance for the apolitical exigencies of the pre-Constantinian church), an undercurrent of pacifism nonetheless exerts power upon the Christian world ever and again, especially amongst, and under the public influence of, Protestant sectarian and perfectionist groups. Judaism has not opened itself to any comparable movement.

Of course, Judaism and the Jewish community have been in the fore-front of teaching and action for peace, and are thus "pacifist" in the original meaning of the term. "The ethical judgment on war, according to Judaism, is that [war] must be eradicated to make human life conform to the divine rule, that those guilty of causing it commit a crime against humanity and a sin against God." This in no way rules out the moral legitimacy and even the obligation of resistance and self-defense against war and aggression.[17] But the Jewish ethic insists that there be no rejoicing in killing, however wicked the enemy. A famous midrash testifies that God rebuked the angels for singing while or because the Egyptian pursuers of the Israelites were drowning. This midrash is contained in the manual of the Israel Defense Forces.[18]

Reference has been made to the presence of obstacles within the Christian corpus to a responsible relating of religious faith to the political order. There is no more formidable case in point than the persisting force of Christian political pacifism, in contrast to Jewish teaching. Political pacifism contends that pacifist methods are capable of fostering justice and reconciliation among political entities. (This view must be carefully distinguished from vocational pacifism, which is a witness of the individual conscience and is often apolitical. Not only American but Israeli law takes into account this latter form of witness.)

The American secretary of state recently made a statement concerning the country's policy in reaction to international terrorism. Reportedly, a certain senior White House official charged that the secretary's "eye-for-an-eye" policy of retaliation is rooted in the Old Testament, and since the United States is "not an Old Testament society, . . . we do not go on the basis of an eye for an eye. We've got a New Testament in this country."[19]

It is hard to imagine a more forceful exemplification than this official's sentiment of the indestructibleness of Christian ideology, its lingering presence in the body politic, its perpetuating of the Jewish-Christian conflict, and its contribution to antisemitism. Its special significance for our interests has to do with the moral confusion within the collective Christian psyche that is pointed to by the official, who, after all, was speaking not in behalf of an ethic for the individual but as the representative of a world-political power. The confusion, long since decried by Reinhold Niebuhr, is between normative Christian behavior at the personal level and the normative responsibilities of social and political praxis. The power of the confusion helps to explain how Christianity has been ever and again beset by a temptation to social and moral irresponsibility. While prevailingly refraining from espousing pacifism as a political ethic, the church at the same time tends to beat its breast in remorse and guilt when it so refrains. Even when the church is accepting or at least living with the necessities and evils of international strife, it yet finds itself called to subsidize the notion that "real Christian behavior" is pacifist. The church is continually tempted to receive political pacifists as blessed ones who truly incarnate "Christian love" rather than judging them for their moral irresponsibilities. This condition obtains much more within Protestant than Catholic Christianity, because the latter is considerably protected against it by virtue of the just-war tradition.

In its response to the White House spokesperson, the Newsletter of today's National Committee on American Foreign Policy builds upon the actual New Testament position:

> Apart from the obvious dangers of injecting theological considerations into the formulation of a country's security interests, the theology that the official did inject is based on fantasy. Had this official read and understood the meaning of the oft-quoted "Love your enemies" in the New Testament, especially in Matthew 5:44 and Luke 6:27, he would have discovered that "Love your enemies" reads . . . love your private enemies, not . . . love your public foes. . . .
>
> The senior White House official's misunderstanding of the New Testament . . . is compounded by his ignorance of the realities and logic of politics. Evidently he does not realize that his blatantly uninformed remarks constitute an invitation to terrorists around the world to strike without fear of retaliation, no matter how destructive of human lives and materiel such strikes may be. If indeed this senior White House official considers his country's security interests to converge with the interests of terrorists, namely, that our common interests would be best served by terrorists attacking America's strategic interests, then Americans really have reason to pray to God and hope that he will protect us from the consequences of the fantasies of some of His humble creations, especially from this senior official of the White House.[20]

Here, as is nascent in the outlook of Jesus, a moral distinction is advocated between individual love for persons and collective political action, as at the same time a naive transition from the one to the other is avoided and the Christian confusion referred to above is prevented. It would be well for the senior White House official to be exposed to a good dose of Israeli policy toward terrorism, an experience that might help open his eyes to what Jesus and the New Testament actually say.

However, Jewish thinking proceeds along a line that, if followed, actually prevents the Christian confusion from getting started. I refer to the doctrine of the sacredness of life. For it is recognized that such sacredness is not consistently honored until it is applied to *every* human life. How could this exclude the life of the individual victim of aggression? Thus does the teaching of the sacredness of all life stand in judgment upon historic Jewish (and other) failures to persevere in it:

> For centuries Jews neglected to pay adequate attention to the advice of those fundamentally nonviolent teachers who said: "If one comes to kill you, anticipate him and kill him first." This statement is not meant to be a call to arms; nor does it require sinking to the level of the Ajax tradition. It suggests that the inadequate response to aggression is morally wrong. Evil has got to be resisted and it is morally wrong not to resist it. For every time evil succeeds because all possible resistance was not offered, its power increases and resistance at a later moment becomes more and more difficult. . . . [To] tolerate evil against oneself, in however mild a form, makes one an accomplice to the act.[21]

In this way the Jewish ethic is able to take Jesus' counsel and bring it to a moral and logical realization that he did not reach. His counsel is of course fully embodied in the concept of voluntary Jewish martyrdom— which is correlative with the ideal of vocational pacifism. Nevertheless, "by Jewish lights, I am under no obligation to turn the other cheek, especially not if I have been unjustly slapped to begin with. The theory that evil should be endured rather than resisted" is not only "an unnatural principle" but "also immoral in that it urges acquiescence in injustice."[22] Through an insistence that even at the personal level unwarranted aggression is to be resisted, Judaism keeps the Christian confusion between individual and social moral standards from ever materializing. The norms of peace, love, and justice apply at *all* levels of human relationships. In this concrete respect, the Jewish ethic is seen to be a higher and more responsible ethic than the Christian ethic.

We are told by one Christian interpreter that the negative attitude toward the State of Israel of many in today's peace movement "can be understood as a modern version of traditional Christian universalism. . . . A 'universalist' ideology has no room for the unique role of the nation

Israel among the world's peoples."[23] A responsible accuracy would have made the writer of these words say the opposite: The negative attitude toward Israel *cannot* be understood as a modern version of traditional Christian universalism, because the peace movement readily makes room for the unique roles of Syria, the Soviet Union, Saudi Arabia, Japan, China, and on and on and on, among the world's peoples. The peace movement's negative attitude toward Israel must therefore come from sources *other than* the one proposed. Careful and disinterested study of the history of the Middle East since 1948 and before will show that the reasons why Arab-Israeli peace is lacking lie not with Israel but with her foes.* Accordingly, the source of the peace movement's antipathy to Israel is not separable from the phenomenon of antisemitism. This brings us to the volatile current confrontation between the Jewish community and the Quakers.

The small Quaker grouping is hardly typical of American Christianity, although it is the most well-known Christian, or at least (largely) gentile, "pacifist" entity in the United States. A pertinent problem for Jews here is that many American Protestant denominational and official groupings, while not themselves officially "pacifist," often behave like Quakers when it comes to their exactions upon Jews.

Quaker ideology is not unrelated to an abiding utopian drive, sometimes repressed and sometimes unrepressed, within the Christian soul (in conspicuous disregard of traditional church teaching upon human sinfulness): the notion that acts of human goodness and love can be counted upon to awaken corresponding behavior in the opponent and enemy. To some degree the Jewish community had itself come under the spell of this illusion—until the night of the *Shoah*.

Upon more careful reflection we may see that traditional Christian utopianism cannot be the secret of Quaker hostility to Israel. For any such interpretation is directly contradicted by Quaker support for terrorism against Israel in the form of the Palestine Liberation Organization. This

---

*Anwar Sadat of Egypt came to the epochal but very practical conclusion that the one effective way to retrieve the Sinai Peninsula and his country's oil resources was to make peace with Israel. Israel eagerly responded to the overture (an overture potentiated only after the Egyptian president had been assured that Israel had helped foil a Libyan plot against him). Here *Realpolitik* was able to offset anti-Israelism and antisemitism. But it is a real question whether Sadat's successors will permit their own self-interest to perpetuate Sadat's policy. At this writing, a powerful anti-Israeli and antisemitic campaign is being conducted in Egypt's government-controlled media.

support is largely implemented through the Quakers' arm, the American Friends Service Committee.[24]

Asia A. Bennett, executive secretary of the AFSC, recently demanded again that the Israelis "negotiate" with the PLO and called for a second Arab state in Palestine.[25] In a piece aptly titled "The Violent Quakers," Robert J. Loewenberg of Arizona State University sums up the situation. "Of all the disillusionments suffered by establishment and liberal Jews" in recent years "none has been more troubling" than the behavior of the Quakers. "Not only have the Quakers, along with other liberals and radicals, taken up the Arab side, the Quakers are the world's stalking horse for the PLO. . . . [Their] obsession with Israel and its destruction has forced all but the most radical Jews to part company with them." Loewenberg asks: How is it possible for these "peacemakers" to support "the world's most notorious band of murderers"? He discerns an explanation in two historical forces: certain strains of sectarian Protestantism, with their incredible incarnationist combination of pacifism and holy terror (cf. the relation between Quakers and Ranters); and the Gnostic contempt for the world and the absolutization of "peace" as the one and only human virtue. (Both these movements are in diametrical opposition to Judaism.) Accordingly, "the record of the American Friends Service Committee in Israel [becomes] one of unabashed support of terrorism and of the murdering of Jews. The Quaker is then a speaker of peace but a supporter of terror. But this contradiction is of the essence of the Gnostic traditions in which Quakerism, and other forms of radical, once heretical Protestantism arose."[26]

It may be necessary to go beyond Professor Loewenberg because his interpretation is open to the query of why the demands of Quaker imperialistic "pacifism" should get restricted to Jews while Arabs are exempt. Subtle and probably unrecognized prejudice may be at work amongst the Quakers (not just against Jews): Are the Quakers somehow insinuating that the Arab people are not fully human? In principle, as human beings Arabs ought to be as subject as any people to the one universal and absolute duty of "peace." Why then is that absolute not demanded of them? Why, for that matter, and on Loewenberg's reasoning, do the Quakers not ally themselves with the cause of Israeli counterterrorism? And why is it that only Jewish and Israeli "militarism" is evil while the imperialist behavior of, for example, Syria is completely passed over?

At this point the storied cynic's comprehensive definition of Christianity—that goy religion which concentrates upon telling the Jewish people to turn the other cheek—shows its pertinence. For it is only the Jews who are to realize the absolute virtue of "peace." Their enemies are wholly absolved from such requirements and are instead encouraged, in effect, to destroy those Jews who have been made vulnerable by perfectionist pressures. Here we see how in the late twentieth century the special problem of "the Friends," as they like to call themselves, is that not alone do they embody the "normal" Christian moral confusion reviewed earlier, together with arguably Christian sectarian and Gnostic proclivities, but also and more particularly they incarnate the closely linked phenomena of Christian hypocrisy and Christian antisemitism. Were this not the case, the Quakers would be insisting upon an identical perfectionism for the foes of Jews that they demand of Jews. They would be calling upon the PLO to desist from its terrorism and engage in reconciliation and peaceableness.

The challenge, therefore, to all Christians is to inquire of themselves whether they too are propagating a double moral standard when they evaluate the Jewish people's responses to aggression. The lesson of the Quakers proves to be paradigmatic of all Christian hostility to Jews. As Eliezer Berkovits writes, "The Christian crime against the Jewish people . . . is the devil's laughter at all those nice Christian affirmations about turning the other cheek and loving one's enemy."[27]

(c) Fetal rights, female rights

On October 7, 1984, shortly before the American national elections, a full-page advertisement appeared in the *New York Times* in the form of a statement sponsored by Catholics For A Free Choice and signed by ninety-seven Catholic professors, theologians, nuns (24), administrators, and others. A footnote indicated that the statement had been signed by many other Catholics, and said that in addition "75 priests, religious and theologians have written that they agree with the Statement but cannot sign because they fear losing their jobs."

The advertisement, identified as "a Catholic statement on pluralism and abortion," was headed, in banner type: "A diversity of opinions regarding abortion exists among committed Catholics." The declaration continued, in part:

Statements of recent Popes and of the Catholic hierarchy have condemned the direct termination of pre-natal life as morally wrong in all instances. There is the mistaken belief in American society that this is the only legitimate Catholic position. . . . A large number of Catholic theologians hold that even direct abortion, though tragic, can sometimes be a moral choice. . . . [There] is no common and constant teaching on ensoulment in Church doctrine, nor has abortion always been treated as murder in canonical history. . . . [It] is necessary that the Catholic community encourage candid and respectful discussion on this diversity of opinion within the Church. . . . [While] recognizing and supporting the legitimate role of the hierarchy in providing Catholics with moral guidance on political and social issues and in seeking legislative remedies to social injustices, we believe that Catholics should not seek the kind of legislation that curtails the legitimate exercise of the freedom of religion and conscience or discriminates against poor women.

The shot was heard round the religious and political world, and not just the Catholic world. On December 18, 1984 the Vatican threatened the twenty-four nuns with expulsion from their orders "on grounds of obstinate insubordination," unless they publicly renounce the statement. At this writing (March 1986) no nun has recanted, and a number of them have declared that they will not do so. As one asked, "How can we retract the truth?" She meant by this the fact of differences among Catholics on abortion.

As against the charges of some of their opponents, the signers were *not* approving the morality of abortion. They were concerned to develop a dialogue among all sides upon a serious and painful question. They wished to point up the great polarization and confusion that exists within as beyond the Catholic community. Beyond this, many of the nuns and their supporters, appealing as Christians to the right of conscience, have decried "the directives of a patriarchal system in which they have no real voice or power," expressed "dismay and shock that the Vatican would respond to their call for dialogue with such potentially harsh penalties," and emphasized that the Vatican reaction imperils the rights of all Roman Catholics to speak freely within the Church.[28]

This episode opens up a number of questions: not alone the morality/immorality of abortion, but the issue of human (female) rights, the legitimacy/illegitimacy of religious authoritarianism, the right of conscience, and freedom of speech in the Christian church. Each of these questions is of the highest relevance to today's Jewish-Christian encounter.

To begin with the final item just listed, freedom of speech, we are

brought back to the two variables identified in chapter one as characteriz-
ing the Christian side of the Jewish-Christian relation as treated in this
book: Christian faith, and Americanness. As we have noted again and
again, American Christianity, not excluding the Catholic Church in this
country, is greatly influenced by modern emphases upon human freedom. The question arises: Is not the appeal of the nuns and their supporters to the right of Roman Catholics to speak freely in the church much
more indicative of, and consistent with, the influence of Americanness
than it is reflective of a moral right inherent to life within the Catholic
Church? Certainly, Vatican Council II pointed up the rights of Christian
conscience.[29] Yet Dennis Crowley appears to describe the actual situation
still obtaining, despite modern reforms, within Catholicism (whether or
not this is how things ought to be):

> A group of Roman Catholic nuns says the Vatican has imperiled the right
> of Catholics to free speech. . . . The Vatican has done nothing of the kind.
> The Vatican merely defends the ancient "magisterium"—the authority to
> teach true doctrine—in the matter of faith and morals, and to claim to
> speak for the church when one supports opinions contrary to the magis-
> terium is as ludicrous as a schoolmaster claiming to teach English when in
> fact he lectures on mathematics. . . .
> There have been others besides these nuns who have departed from the
> discipline of Rome while maintaining a nostalgic attachment to the notion
> of Catholicity: they are known as Protestants.[30]

Perhaps of equal significance, therefore, to the banner heading of the
New York Times advertisement concerning differences among Catholics
on abortion was the footnote in the tiniest of print telling of the non-
signers who feared the loss of their jobs. Of course, all religious, social,
and political entities maintain measures of discipline, authority, and
control. There are variations on a scale from highly authoritarian and
collectivist types to highly democratic and individualist types. These are
differences in degree. But in the specific case we are discussing there is
also an essential difference in kind: The effort to control the thinking and
behavior of these American Catholic leaders has its locus beyond the
United States, an impossibility for the Protestant and the Jewish communities.

Furthermore, Dennis Crowley's observation does not wholly silence all
questions: Is genuine dissent to be entirely excluded within the bounds of
the Catholic Church? Is the "truth" to be determined exclusively by an
ecclesiastical body? Just what is left for "freedom of conscience"? The

answers to these questions have very great import in relations between Roman Catholic Christianity on the one side and Protestants and Jews on the other side. This is seen in a query put by one of the nuns: "What is to be the future of ecumenical and interreligious dialogue?"

Finally, the Catholic hierarchy's threat to "demote" the nuns to lay status is typical—some of the nuns have made this point—of a traditional dualism according to which lay people are spiritually and morally inferior to the "religious" and the clergy. This is to be contrasted to the insistence in Judaism that there is a single lay status for all Jews and that all people are equal (a position that is, however, flouted by certain rabbinic claimants many more times than once). As for Protestantism, that movement falls, as ever, between the two stools, due to its diversity. There is great stress upon lay people and lay dignity, yet clericalism is hardly absent from the Protestant world.

Let us return to the question of abortion. The Catholic-Jewish conflict is transparent here, as is, for the most part, the Catholic-Protestant conflict. We say "for the most part" in light of a recent development among some Christians who evidently would wish to be known as Protestants but who are absolutists against abortion, contrary to the traditional Protestant position of recent times. Liberal Protestants tend to be relatively permissive on this matter; increasing numbers of evangelical Protestants are today tending in the other direction. This parallels the situation in Jewish circles, where non-Orthodox Jews tend to be relatively less restrictive than Orthodox Jews. Protestantism as a whole has placed great stress upon the quality of life and the welfare of the family, in ways that follow the general Jewish viewpoint.

There is essential Jewish concern for the wellbeing of the mother, not alone in a physical sense but spiritually and psychologically. Halakhic Judaism permits abortion, and even morally demands it, in such circumstances as adultery, incest, rape, and malformed fetuses. The mother's life, as an actualized life, takes precedence over the potential life of the fetus. Judaism rejects the notion of abortion on demand* and as a device for population control. But abortion is not murder. Were it considered murder, "a mother would not be allowed to have an abortion even to save her life, which is obviously not the case."[31]

---

*The Supreme Court decision in *Roe v. Wade* (1973) does not positively endorse abortion. It sanctions a pregnant woman's decision on the matter, in consultation with her physician, at least during the first period of pregnancy.

The talmudic principle that no human life is inherently superior or inferior to another life is of aid in choosing between the life of the mother and the survival of the fetus only because the fetus is not held to embody actual human life. More precisely, the issue of which life is to take precedence becomes a non-question. Were the opposite view ever to prevail—the fetus *is* an actual human life—then in instances where the mother faces no serious problems, the talmudic principle of human equality and the sanctity of life could be utilized, I should think, as a ground for illegitimizing abortion.

Any distinction between potential and actual life respecting the fetus is wholly unacceptable to traditional Catholic ecclesiastical authority. The rights of the fetus or the child take precedence over those of the mother, even if she will die. The reason is strictly religious: new souls command an inviolable right of eligibility for salvation under the aegis of this life's duties and opportunities. Under a new code of Catholic canon law completed in 1983, abortion is numbered among grave sins punishable by automatic excommunication. This applies not only to the person having the abortion but to the individual performing it.

To conclude our brief treatment of the theme "fetal rights, female rights," here are a few highly debatable contentions for discussion within the Christian-Jewish meeting:

(i) Is not a moral and practical distinction required between religious opposition to abortion and the legal prohibition of abortion in a pluralist nation? Today there appears to be too much conflict on this subject in the populace as a whole for the problem to be resolvable by legislation.

(ii) In point of fact, the board of the National Coalition of American Nuns is as opposed to abortion as anyone; the only question is whether there are times when, lamentably, abortions may be called for.

(iii) Today's womanist reformers in the back of the Catholic Church (some of them males) are expressing the view that the anti-mother policy of their Church may well be a reflection of male chauvinism and anti-womanism. It is extremely doubtful that such a policy would ever have triumphed had ecclesiastical authority been female rather than male. More than one leader in the National Coalition of American Nuns contends that the recent politicizing of the abortion issue by Church authorities is much more than a device for refusing to concede the great diversity amongst Catholics on this matter. Is it not also a method for perpetuating male power in the Church? Spokespersons for the coalition find it significant, in this regard, that several bishops attacked a female candidate for the vice presidency of the United States, herself a Catholic, for her supposed laxity on abortion—she was in fact very traditionalist on the subject—at the same time that they carefully refrained from censuring male Catholic politicians holding a view identical to hers. Is not the Church's present ideological campaign upon abortion thereby seen to be inseparable from its ideology upon women? A judgment by the 2,000-member National Coalition of American Nuns coheres with this point: "We reject the sexism which leads the [U.S.] bishops to believe that they alone have the right and wisdom to make decisions about the morality of a woman's existential choice about pregnancy when that choice differs from the bishops' theoretical one."[32]

(iv) So-called pro-life people concentrate upon the life of the defenseless fetus. That position itself raises questions of ideological taint. Are not other interests involved than the defense of innocent life? Are these people prepared to support the vast social instrumentalities and public budget required to sustain the human lives not aborted? What about post-fetal rights? Are the "pro-life" advocates males? Are females involved? If the latter, is there a sense in which these women are negating the obligations and opportunities of their own human freedom? Are they not selling themselves to the traditional attempt of males to rule over human reproduction? Males know nothing about pregnancy, yet try to control reproduction. The consequences of pregnancy, particularly out of wedlock, fall almost completely upon women.

(v) One possible way to live with the conflict between fetal rights and female rights is to recognize that an unqualified prohibition of abortion of necessity flouts female rights while the honoring of female rights does not of necessity flout fetal rights. "Pro-life" is closed to "pro-choice" but "pro-choice" is open to "pro-life." Praxis for the sake of the children is defended and strongly counseled. This point is in accord with the rejection by the National Coalition of American Nuns (October 1984) of the notion that to be pro-choice is to be pro-abortion. Furthermore, as Madonna Kolbenschlag attests, "assuring women's moral freedom and establishing a social policy that provides them with *real* options so that they can take responsibility for life and make authentic decisions of conscience ought to be the priority for both the prolife and the prochoice groups."[33]

The moral issue here receives continued attention in chapter seven.

7

$\blacklozenge$

Enter the Women's Movement

> Women's experience will be the hermeneutic of
> the future.
>
> —Madonna Kolbenschlag

We devote a separate chapter to the next theme because the women's movement* may well prove to have as much significance for the Jewish-Christian relation as the Holocaust and the refounding of the State of Israel—probably, in the long run, greater significance. Women constitute half or more of the Jewish and Christian populations, a fact as potentially momentous as it is obvious.

Two coauthors, Deborah McCauley, a Christian, and Annette Daum, a Jew, bring home the truth that a most weighty handicap of the Jewish-Christian dialogue to date is its overwhelmingly patriarchal and androcentric character and thrust. A prevailing consequence is the domination of problems of exclusivity over testimonies to inclusivity.[1]

The menace of sexism raised its head toward the end of the previous chapter. As a means of transition to this new chapter, it seems fitting, for the sake of structural continuity but also of substance, to utilize as a concrete point of departure the possible link, hinted at in the last section of chapter six, between certain church policies and the anti-womanism that has perforce mothered the women's movement. A second concrete means of introduction will be the issue of ordination.

---

*The phrase "women's movement" is not the best since the maltreatment of individual females hardly waits for them to become grown women. "Female movement" is infelicitous. "Feminist movement" sounds ideological, even though in fact the movement is not that in any negative or disparaging sense. Part of the polemic of women's liberation is that women, while feminine, are much more than feminine.

I

In recent years the fetus, normally an invisible reality that lives off a woman's body, has become highly visible, while the pregnant woman, readily seen by the naked eye, has been sentenced to invisibility. This is nothing new. The invisibility of women is a staple of patriarchal society, including Jewish and Christian society.

The National Coalition of American Nuns rejects the attitude that "denies personhood to the woman and bestows it on the fetus."[2] These nuns testify—many of them speaking out of intimate experience striving to succor abused, poor, and downtrodden women—that the abortion of women's dignity is as cruel as, or more cruel than, any form of abortion. They insist that the issue of fetal abortion is inseparable from the struggle for the rights of women.* Knowingly or not, they are applying the rabbinic dictum, "No woman is required to build the world by destroying herself" (counsel that is scorned not only within Christianity but within Judaism itself).

One spokesperson for the nuns' coalition emphasizes that the woman whose authority over the reproductive dimension of her life is taken away, a dimension that is central to her existence, is being robbed of command over her life as a whole. She is being treated as a non-person. True humanness means freedom, means choice. The attack upon choice is an attack upon the humanity of women. The same spokesperson asks, Why is it that bishops and priests so seldom refer to the procreative obligations posed by *male* sexuality? (A like question may be addressed to some rabbis and Protestant ministers.)

The precipitous rush of the issue of abortion to the center of the American socio-political arena is a rather evident symptom of profound male anxiety over the rise of female empowerment. (How else are we to account for the recent rash of bombings of abortion clinics?) Opposition to "pro-choice" and to the Equal Rights Amendment together seems to come from

---

*The women's movement in the Roman Catholic Church goes back to the early 1960s and the Second Vatican Council. Contrary to what male Vatican officialdom wants people to think, that movement is independent of more recent American liberation movements.

those who have the most to lose from the empowerment of women, either psychologically and politically, or in terms of authority or financial resources. Thus, for many men there is a consistency between their privileged position in the family and society and the value placed on fetal life, over which they have no intrinsic control. This may help to explain the curious contradiction in the views expressed by some churchmen and politicians who are so intransigent on the issue of abortion, over which men have no physical control, and so tolerant of killing in war, over which men have always had control. . . . And in the impasse, other issues—child care, research on contraception, sex education, and increasingly, the specter of reproductive technology—are neglected or distorted. The prospect of what some have called "the colonization of the womb" and the enormity of the problems looming on the horizon should stir us all to outrage at the concentration of so much energy and so many resources, so much sound and fury, on the abortion issue. It reminds one of those who, after World War II and Hiroshima and Nagasaki, were still arguing over whether or not submarine warfare was moral.[3]

Our second mode of introduction to the women's movement is the subject of ordination. Not long ago an American Catholic priest was heard to lament that clerical ordination, which requires the possession of a penis, simultaneously cuts off, in a perverse way, any future employment of that organ in the procreation of children. One available if revolting comfort for the priest is the judgment of a Catholic bishop in Nebraska that Scripture is demeaned whenever a woman reads it in church. Current Vatican regulations prohibit females from serving at the altar and reserve to males any formal entry into the lay ministries of reader and acolyte.[4] An editorial in the largely though not solely Protestant journal *Christianity and Crisis* finds that "exclusion of women from ordination in the Catholic Church is the most basic institutional instrument of marginalization still extant, at least in the Western world—not because it denies individual women any chance to exercise sacerdotal ministry, but because it says that *all* women are *incapable* of full participation in the life of the Catholic community."[5]

While Judaism knows nothing of a sacerdotal ministry, rabbis constitute its pivotal leaders, filling today the decisive functions of teaching, scholarship, conduct of worship and sacred rites, preaching, counseling, and administration. Although Orthodox Judaism does not suffer from the same physiological contradiction that is referred to in the previous paragraph, penis-possession remains a *sine qua non* for its rabbinate. That is to say, female rabbis are said to be in violation of *halakhah*. The history of the rabbinate, the Catholic priesthood, and the Protestant ministry is, until the innovations of recent years, a story of male dominance over and exploitation of females.

Reform Judaism in the U.S.A. has ordained women since 1972, when the first female rabbi was graduated from Hebrew Union College. After a protracted struggle, Conservative Judaism altered its sexist policy, on the ground that *halakhah* is a dynamic reality that permits changes with the times. In late 1983 the Jewish Theological Seminary of America opened its rabbinical program to women, and in early 1985 the Rabbinical Assembly voted to admit women to full membership upon ordination. Reconstructionist Judaism freely ordains women. Many Protestant denominations provide for the ordination of females. In 1983 a resolution passed the Southern Baptist Convention rejecting the ordination of women to the ministry. However, to this date more than 300 Southern Baptist women have been ordained.

Provision for female ordination will continue to have limited meaning until women rabbis and ministers gain equality of opportunity and acceptance. Today relatively few attain senior posts. Their remuneration is markedly lower than that of males. Many of them end up as assistants, youth directors, and educational administrators, or are relegated to small churches or congregations. Very few hold leadership positions. Large numbers of women leave the ministry and some leave the rabbinate. One primary reason for this in Protestant denominations is a failure on the part of parishioners and local church staff people to acknowledge authority when it is represented in women. The social psychopathology is transparent. A female Presbyterian minister in Omaha reports that of the twelve women in her 1978 seminary class, she is the only one remaining in the parish ministry. There are 1,326 Presbyterian ministers in Iowa, Minnesota, Wisconsin, Nebraska, North Dakota, and South Dakota. Of these, eighty-six are women. Fewer than fifty of them are in the parish ministry, and as of early 1985 many of the latter were in the process of leaving a parish setting and looking for secular employment.[6]

With most of the world's religions, Judaism and Christianity share a history of and ideology for the special treatment of females. (Cf. the Nazi euphemism *Sonderbehandlung*, special treatment of Jews.) In the case of women, the special treatment ranges from idealization to calumniation, from virtual divinization to demonization. The close affinity within these diametrically opposite characteristics is disclosed in the fact that males are the ones who invent them, and the labels are never assigned to males as males. Thus, there are "fallen women" but of course no fallen men. Ann Patrick Ware comments aptly upon a recent seminar called "Images of Women in Christian and Jewish Traditions": The very title "confirms the perception that what women are and do is not normative but derivative. Can one imagine a session entitled 'Images of Men . . .'? Men are men, but women must represent something. Women's actions, words, appearance constitute an 'image' of women, not a reality."[7]

Men are men, but women are something other than women. They are emotional, irrational, weak, frivolous, of insatiable sexual appetite, and sensuous. (The last three on the list are found in the Talmud.) "All 'images' of women, even the most favorable, work to the disadvantage of women. Whether 'woman' is perceived as temptress, siren, seductress, sex-symbol, clinging vine, Amazon, teacher and upholder of society's morals, the hand that rocks the cradle and thus rules the world, the power behind the throne—in every instance, the image places on women the burden of responsibility for what is wrong with the world. In this way, the burden of the image put upon women is not unlike the burden that society puts upon the State of Israel—making it out to be the sole cause of trouble in the Middle East, either because it is so innately wicked or because, called to be better than any other nation it is failing in its call."[8]

In a word, women are "the other," those who are on trial—not unlike Jews, not unlike God.

II

The women's movement and the issues it raises converge upon the encounter of Jews and Christians in many discrete and decisive ways. Several of these may be singled out.

(a) The Christian church whose history is suffused with antisemitism and triumphalism has always been a male-dominated community; conversion to womanism may have implications for the struggle against antisemitism.

Would things have become as bad had the church not been male sexist? An affirmative answer assumes that males and females are equally adept at such a sin as antisemitism—and that protestation is a long, long way from being convincing. In fact, some womanists discern close links between Christian imperialist antisemitism and characteristically male chauvinist behavior. The whole structure of Christian supersession was erected by males. The Holocaust, for all its unprecedented and unique character, and for all its ensnaring of women participants, is at one with the common and perennial infamy of male wars and male destructiveness.

Letty Cottin Pogrebin, editor of *Ms.*, reckons with the bond between antisemitism and antiwomanism. She proposes a pristine criterion for political friendship: "If you are not an ally of women, you cannot be considered an ally of Jews." There are three reasons for this: Since some of all women are Jews and half of all Jews are women, "what is bad for women cannot be good for Jews"; women and Jews together constitute "the other" vis-à-vis those who hold the dominant power in American society: white, male Christians; and "because my political allies must protect my most basic self-interests. I am a Jew *and* a woman. . . . Since I cannot split myself in half, it is impossible for me to support people or policies that ensure my freedom and safety as a Jew but do not *simultaneously* ensure my freedom and safety as a woman—and vice versa."

With these guidelines at hand, Pogrebin assesses the Ally Quotients (A.Q.) of several political and religious leaders. She compares and contrasts two members of the Christian clergy, Jesse Jackson and Jerry Falwell. Jackson's anti-Israel "evenhandedness" and antisemitic slurs seem to lower his A.Q. against Falwell's expressed support of Israel (to be sure, on Christian terms). However, in contrast to Jackson,

> Falwell and his ilk have made no secret of their moral imperialism: they intend *by law*, not just public suasion, to "Christianize America," impose prayer in public schools, revitalize family patriarchy, outlaw reproductive freedom and give the fetus more rights than the woman in whose body it exists.
>
> They have proved their enmity by word and deed. In comparison, Jackson is at worst an indiscreet bigot, like millions of Christians—black and white—and at best an unknown quantity, a man whose commitments on the Jewish question have yet to be tested. But on the woman question, Jackson has come a long way: he has moved from anti-choice to pro-choice on reproductive rights, and from the knee-jerk male supremacy of the old black power movement to a position of sensitivity and advocacy on women's needs. I believe he and his supporters can be similarly sensitized on Jewish needs.

In sum, there is much hope for Jackson and little or no hope for Falwell. Attitudes to women are established as the litmus test for actual and potential Christian attitudes to Jews.[9] The abandonment of Christian imperialism as such means hope for both the male acceptance of women as equals and the Christian acceptance of Jews as equals.

(b) The one prison cell of sexism is shared by Jewish and Christian constituencies.

Rachel Adler writes:

> It is not unusual for committed Jewish women to be uneasy about their position as Jews. It was to cry down our doubts that rabbis developed their pre-packaged orations on the nobility of motherhood; the glory of child-birth; and modesty, the crown of Jewish womanhood. I have heard them all. I could not accept those answers for two reasons. First of all, the answers did not accept *me* as a person. . . . Second, the answers were not really honest ones. . . .
>
> Ultimately our problem stems from the fact that we are viewed in Jewish law and practice as peripheral Jews. The category in which we are general-ly placed includes women, children and Canaanite slaves. Members of this category are exempt from all positive commandments which occur within time limits. These commandments would include hearing the shofar on Rosh HaShanah, eating in the Sukkah, praying with the lulav, praying the three daily services, wearing tallit and t'fillin, and saying Sh'ma. In other words, members of this category have been "excused" from most of the positive symbols which, for the male Jew, hallow time, hallow his physical being, and inform both his myth and his philosophy. . . .
>
> All of the individuals in this tri-partite category I have termed peripheral Jews. Children, if male, are full Jews *in potentio*. Male Canaanite slaves, if freed, become full Jews, responsible for all the mitzvot and able to count in a minyan. Even as slaves, they have the b'rit mila, the covenant of circumcision, that central Jewish symbol, from which women are an-atomically excluded. It is true that in Jewish law women are slightly more respected than slaves, but that advantage is outweighed by the fact that only women can never grow up, or be freed or otherwise leave the category.[10]

Corresponding Christian discrimination against and exploitation of women have already been noted. Added citations from Ann Patrick Ware may be set alongside the words of Rachel Adler:

> In the Hebrew Bible only males are full-fledged members of the Jewish people, but Israel, when unfaithful, is portrayed as a harlot. The "New"

Testament, which hints at the equality of the sexes by having all enter into the covenant by baptism, ends the revelation by presenting a vision of white-garbed men enjoying proximity to the throne of God because they have not "defiled" themselves with women. . . . The revised [Catholic] canon law (composed by men), which has rectified some of the grosser inequities in speaking of women, still puts the most severe ecclesiastical penalty, excommunication, on abortion (a woman's decision) but not on murder, rape, incest (mainly acts of men). . . . Papal statements refer frequently to "the nature of women" and are full of advice to women about fulfilling their nature. As long as women are perceived to have a special nature and not human nature, they are perceived as a deviant species.[11]

A parallel may be discerned under our second heading to Letty Cottin Pogrebin's correlating of antisemitism and antiwomanism. From a Christian womanist perspective, the relative non-openness of Orthodox Judaism to Christians in contrast to openness to Christians in non-Orthodox Judaism correlates with the antiwomanism that distinguishes Orthodox Judaism from non-Orthodox Judaism.

(c) The rampancy of sexism within the Jewish tradition and Judaism— typified by the inequalities suffered by women in today's Israel[12]—helps offset, substantively as well as psychologically, a stress upon the moral asymmetry of the Jewish-Christian relation, a stress ordinarily necessitated, as we have seen, by the presence and power of Christian antisemitism and supersessionism.

Jews who are tempted to self-righteousness by Christian offenses may perhaps be reminded that all is hardly well in the Jewish world. The synagogue shares with the church a liturgy and imagery that, very largely, is still sexually exclusivist. A young graduate-student friend from Wisconsin recently converted from Christianity to Judaism. She said to my wife and me, "At last, I am part of a tradition of which I can be proud." Comparatively taken, her testimony is faithful to the historical record. An original impetus for her decision was her distress over the immorality of Christian antisemitism. However, more than one Jewish woman cannot feel as she does. Christians, out of disillusionment with their faith or through happy encounters with Jewish people, are sometimes tempted to idealize Judaism or the Jewish community. Soon or late they must come hard against a still-prevalent sexism there. If the greatest evil of historic Christianity is its antisemitism, a grievous wrong within Judaism concerns the status of women. In point of fact, is not sexism the only serious count to be entered against Judaism?

As Jewish feminists again and again point out, no problem is more conspicuous or stubborn or serious than the rite of circumcision, involving as it does, traditionally and contemporaneously, "*the* physical sign of being in covenant with God."[13] If, as the Mishnah states, Abraham was not called perfect, i.e., a completed human being, until he was circumcised, it follows that women have no way to become completed human beings.* (Christian baptism is free of the taint of sexism. Here is a place where the moral asymmetry between Judaism and Christianity is reversed.)

However wholly unacceptable is the apostle Paul's Christian supersessionism, his emphasis upon the ultimate irrelevance of circumcision may be interpreted as a strangely prevenient Christian judgment upon Judaism. This is said strictly in the context of the discrete problem of sexism and not at all with respect to the truth and place of Torah as a whole. Furthermore, Paul's emphasis allies him, in an astonishing way, with womanism. (I say "astonishing" because Paul was anything but a womanist.) What I have in mind is the apostle's allusion to Jews and gentiles: "Neither circumcision counts for anything nor uncircumcision, but keeping the commandments of God" (I Cor. 7:19). This may be applied to our present subject.

In a biblical frame of reference, Paul is on the face of it talking nonsense, since circumcision *means* keeping God's commandments (Gen. 17:10). But in the late twentieth century the apostle's contention, applied to a Jewish feminist hermeneutic, gains contemporary power and application. In Romans Paul declares:

> If a man who is uncircumcised keeps the precepts of the law, will not his uncircumcision be regarded as circumcision? . . . For he is not a real Jew who is one outwardly, nor is true circumcision something external and physical. He is a Jew who is one inwardly, and real circumcision is a matter of the heart, spiritual and not literal. His praise is not from men but from God. (Rom. 2:26, 28–29)

The plain implication of the previously quoted words of Rachel Adler is that the observance of Torah and the commandments is a right wholly

---

*McCauley and Daum refer briefly to the pros and cons of such alternative practices as the ritual breaking of an infant female's hymen and ear piercing as a symbol for covenant relationship. The latter accords symbolically with both the command to hear the word of God and with the ritual shedding of blood.

inherent to Jewish women. Paying full heed to her lament over the marginalizing of Jewish females, we may venture to rewrite, in her behalf and theirs, the Pauline affirmation:

> Clearly a woman of Israel remains uncircumcised. But through her honoring of the precepts of Torah, this uncircumcision is seen to have no consequence. Her uncircumcision is to be deemed the same as circumcision. . . . For she is not a real Jew who is one outwardly, nor is true circumcision something that only males can achieve. She is a Jew who is one inwardly, and real circumcision means being treated as a human being, with full dignity and rights. Her praise is not from men but from God.

In contemporary parlance, the way that Jewish men and Jewish women are made equal adherents of Judaism is through equally keeping the Torah. "Neither circumcision nor uncircumcision counts for anything." The answer to "uncircumcision" is found, and can only be found, in the unqualified opening of Torah-observance to women. (We are led to an incredible conclusion, to be taken not literally but with the seriousness of laughter: Paul never knew it but he was, preveniently, though only at this single point, an unwitting supporter of today's Jewish feminism.)

(d) Antisemitism is by no means absent from the women's movement.

This circumstance helps counteract, or ought to, any impetus to idealize that movement or women—or, better, it points up the powerful impact of patriarchal destructiveness upon the psychological-intellectual condition and praxis of women. Historically speaking, the intensifying presence of antisemitism in the women's movement "is rooted in anti-Judaic male theology of the past, and was incorporated into the movement for suffrage in 19th century America." An example of the latter is the influential and blatantly antisemitic work of Elizabeth Cady Stanton, *The Women's Bible* (1895). Some Christian feminists "have fallen prey to the ancient masculine trap of triumphalism." Judaism and Jewry have "always been the primary 'Other' onto which Christianity has projected those parts of itself to which it will not lay claim. In this scenario, Judaism becomes the bad parent whom Christianity as the adult child blames and punishes for those parts of its personality it does not like and for which it refuses to accept responsibility. The phenomenon of patriarchal projection is made manifest in Christian and post-Christian feminist writings which either explicitly or implicitly blame Judaism for the initial and formative development of the misogyny and sexism we experience in both Christianity and Western civilization."[14]

This particular variation within antisemitism is exemplified in the misrepresentation found amongst some non-Jewish feminists concerning the binding of Isaac by his father Abraham, wherein the "sacrifice" of the child is transformed into a renunciation of matriarchal protection in the furtherance of a patriarchal system. The plain truth, of course, is that the story teaches the *rejection* of child-sacrifice.[15] Womanist antisemitism is also brought to the surface and compounded via the claim that Jesus was a feminist. True, he was also a male. To date, the feminist claim for him is seldom utilized, as it could very well be, in order to show that Jesus' evident sympathy for women was typifying a moral impulse strictly within Judaism. Most often the claim concerning Jesus becomes an ideological stress upon the faults of traditional Jewish behavior, as against the presumed virtues of the central figure in Christianity. One complicating factor, which probably does not help things, is that it is sometimes Christian males who put forward the (alleged) feminism of Jesus in (alleged) contrast to Jesus' peers.[16] Withal, the "feminism" of Jesus was soon to be buried by a church whose sexism exceeded, if anything, the continuing sexism of the Jewish world.

In this same connection reference is made to a lectionary recently prepared through the National Council of Churches. The original charge to the working committee was "to eliminate anti-Semitism as well as sexism." The first part of the charge was dropped as falling outside (*sic!*) the competency of the scholars. As McCauley and Daum comment, a result of the exclusion has been "the preparation of yet another Christian feminist document that will bring us into the next century perpetuating anti-Judaic scripture readings and interpretations in Christian churches."[17] One particularly devastating "improvement" is a change from "His blood be on us and our children" (Matt. 27:25) to "Jesus' blood be on us and our children." The alteration, made with the best of conscious intentions, will, as Daum puts it, "inadvertently provide fuel to fire the charge of deicide that has caused centuries of persecution of the Jewish people."[18]

Many of the most promising revolutionary movements are unable, or do not wish, to keep themselves free of antisemitism. In our present, specific context the antisemitism of the women's movement recapitulates the moral asymmetry that applies between Jewishness and Christianness as a whole. However, in fairness it has to be remembered that some of the antisemitism in the women's movement comes from people who have abandoned Christianity.

(e) The heart of the women's movement is its dialectical insistence that women have rights as women and they have rights as human beings, and that these two kinds of right are inseparable and must be respected as one.

We have here a generalizing proposition that yet allows for discrepancies, conflicts, and differing emphases within the movement itself. A close and important parallel is seen to the overall warrant of the Jewish minority community, with its assertion that at one and the same time, Jews have rights as Jews and they have rights as human beings.

This dialectic as a whole is saying that female bodily existence is at once of total relevance and total irrelevance. It is totally relevant because woman possesses essential authority over the reproductive and other womanly dimensions of her life. But female bodily existence is also irrelevant because there is the avowal by more and more women that to fixate their meaning and destiny as human beings upon their anatomy is intolerable. Again, women are not to be prostituted to some social ideology, as in the pervasive drive of today, traceable to the residual force of the Puritan work-ethic and goaded on by capitalist mentality, to turn women into business people and professionals. The institution of the working woman becomes licit when that is the woman's wish and the woman's affirmed duty.

Do Jewish feminism and Christian feminism undermine family life? On the Jewish side, is the women's movement a special threat to Jewish survival, which has been so largely sustained by the family? The Jewish womanist rejoinder is disarmingly simple: Let women deal with these questions on a par with men. Christian womanists give the same rejoinder. The womanist assertion that all human beings are equally imaged of God does not deny that there may be special female roles, obligations, or contributions, any more than it denies these things for males. In fact, the doctrinaire rejection of these special considerations is among the elements intrinsic to sexism. The opposite of sexism is freedom to be one's *self*, as a female, or male, human being. Women are women, and women are human beings: this is the twofold right that merely duplicates—and authorizes—human realization by males since time immemorial. Women are autonomous over their own lives: here is the simple message of the women's movement. The power of this message for Jewish integrity and freedom in general and Christian integrity and freedom in general cannot be overestimated.

(f) The Jewish-Christian-feminist relation spawns an alliance of potentially massive power.

True, Jewish womanists are divided over whether the community of Jewish faith can still claim their loyalty, and the same division is found among Christian womanists respecting the church. Jewish feminists have the additional burden of dealing with those Christian feminists who refuse to face up to and renounce the anti-Jewishness of some feminist writers. This could serve to drive Jewish womanists outside the institutional network of feminist scholarship and action.[19] The good news is that the cause of equality and justice for females is creating many opportunities for collaborative, shared effort amongst half or more of the total population of the churches and synagogues. Indeed, there is no reason why males cannot come over to the right side in the battle and enjoy the festivities.

III

Let us dwell, lastly, upon a possibly creative and redeeming contribution from within the women's movement to the Jewish-Christian meeting, with special emphasis upon Jewish-Christian reconciliation. This will involve brief forays into the meaning of revolution; the disparity (once again) between Jewishness and Christianness; the problem of male saviorhood; the encumbrance within Christian feminism; the consanguinity of antisemitic, Christological, and sexist idolatries; and the final nemesis for antisemitism. We shall witness the convergence of these variables upon the redeeming reality of Jewish womanism.

Three major attitudes vie for dedication:

> *Anti-womanist ideology*. Here the androcentric tradition is inviolable and true. Contemporary womanist awareness and demands are no more than illicit self-exaltation.
> *Dialectical reform*. Neither the androcentric tradition nor the new womanist awareness is to be wholly accepted or wholly rejected. Justice is to be sought between whatever is valid in the tradition and whatever is compelling in womanist awareness and demands.
> *Pro-womanist revolution*. The androcentric tradition is evil and to be totally rejected. Womanist awareness and demands have true authority.[20]

A tripartite structure of traditionalism, reform, and revolution may be applied in the treatment of all sorts of social issues. In what follows, the androcentric tradition is repudiated, and the third alternative is embodied in ways that stand in judgment upon the second. One complicating point requires mention. The difference between radical womanists, who tend to have little hope for religious faith, and reforming womanists, who are more hopeful for faith, impinges upon the differences between Jewishness and Christianness: Are the people who are involved Jews or are they Christians? As we noted early on, the loss or absence of faith does not exclude a Jew from Jewishness whereas Christian faith is requisite to Christianness. Accordingly, a radical Jewish womanist and a radical Christian womanist, as just characterized, are not in identical predicaments vis-à-vis their respective communities, nor do they, accordingly, have the same potential opportunities.

In some circles of the women's movement Pope John Paul II's argumentation upon why only males can be priests, viz., it was in male form that God became incarnate, is turned against itself. The argument is viewed as self-refuting and self-condemning. Is not the best evidence of the untruthfulness of the Incarnation-claim its pretension to male saviorhood? Insofar as males are radically exploitive of women, how could a male ever be their savior? A disease does not cure itself. The androcentric character of the Catholic priesthood (as of the Orthodox Jewish rabbinate) is a violation of the revealed truth that all human beings are made in the image of God.[21]

There are resources within the women's movement for meliorating Christianity's intolerance of Judaism and Judaism's (lesser) intolerance of Christianity. Female inclusivity is a winsome-powerful weapon against male exclusivity.[22] Yet, as we have seen, Christian feminism is itself not free of the taint of antisemitism that afflicts Christianity as such. Accordingly, our present subject requires a much more discrete and much deeper approach.

J. Coert Rylaarsdam states: "For Christians dialogue with Israel cannot really begin until they have dealt with their own problem."[23] By the Christians' "own problem" Rylaarsdam means: Judaism and the Jewish people. Dorothee Sölle finds Rylaarsdam's statement especially relevant to Christian women as "heirs to a religious tradition that, as part of its ethos, disinherits the female. Our relationship to a tradition that claims universalism is ambiguous because of the oppressive character of this very tradition for one half of humanity."[24] On the Jewish side, we have the parallel of a tradition that claims to exalt justice and sanctify life but still largely fails to honor those norms when it comes to females.

Professor Sölle draws together, from a Christian perspective, the two problems, the Christian affliction of Jews and the Christian affliction of women. "In a Christology 'from above,' Jesus no longer represents only 'the word of God,' spoken to us non-Jews and mediating the covenant between God and the goyim; instead he is the exclusive savior who has fulfilled 'once and for all' what God wants us to do. The result has been, overwhelmingly, a Christological perfectionism that leads believers into what Bonhoeffer called 'cheap grace,' in which Christ elicits admiration instead of imitation and in which he is severed from both his Jewish religious tradition and his prophesy of the yet-to-be-realized messianic kingdom."[25] There is the radical Christian womanism that cuts through the chains of a "savior" who does not save, one in whom, and in whose maleness, women are in fact victimized. The avowedly Protestant Christian feminist Dorothee Sölle and the avowedly post-Christian feminist Mary Daly can embrace in their repugnance for what the latter calls "Christolatry," the "idolatrous worship of a supernatural, timeless divine being who has little in common with the Jewish Jesus of Nazareth."[26]

Within and through the very struggle of Christian women *and men* against the Christological victimization of women, there is also carried forward the struggle against the victimization of Jews. The radical womanist attack upon the idolatrous deification of a male human being as alleged savior constitutes a unique and unprecedented world-historical (world-transforming) event, equaling or excelling the Holocaust and a restored State of Israel. The reason for saying this is that the event cuts not merely in one epochal moral direction but in two: It attacks the deification of not just any human being but the specific deification that created anti-Jewish supersessionism; and it attacks the world-destroying sexism that came to penetrate Christianity (because of *this* male "savior") in continuity with the sexism of Judaism. The inner bond between Christian antisemitism and Christian antiwomanism is disclosed. The one single root cause of both these phenomena in the Christian world is the triumphalism of a male "savior." The whole of Christian history exhibits a single affliction, with two faces. There is the idolatrous divinizing of a human being, and there is the idolatrous male-izing of divinity.

If anti-Judaism and antisemitism are, as Rosemary Ruether says, the left hand of Christology, androcentric sexism stands at its right hand.

Thus does the radical women's revolution become a resource, if an unintended one, for vanquishing the historic Christian derogation of things Jewish. This is not to imply that the women's movement is a means to an end. Were that the case, we should remain in the abyss of the exploitation of females. The contribution of the women's movement to overcoming Jewish-Christian moral asymmetry is an event of free grace, and it is to be received and celebrated as such.

Yet we are still confronted by a considerably sexist Judaism. If that faith has always kept itself immune to human divinization, it has hardly escaped the sin of sexism. And the thoroughly Jewish Jesus remains, after all, a male. A final tragedy for the Christian church would be its deliverance from Christological idolatry only to land in the idolatries of a continuing Jewish sexism. This suggests that the real hope and real future for Christianity, as also for the Jewish ideal of justice and the sanctification of life, are linked to the future and the prosperity of the Jewish feminist movement. For only the empowerment of Jewish womanism—which, unlike Christian womanism, is not hung up psychologically and spiritually upon the problematic of the saviorhood/nonsaviorhood of a male being—can overcome, at one and the same time, all three of the evils that assail us: Christian supersessionist and exclusivist imperialism against Jews and Judaism; the antisemitism of the women's movement; and the mortal sin of Christian and Jewish androcentrism. Therefore, to the extent that Christian feminism frees itself from traditional Christian anti-Jewish, patriarchal triumphalism, it becomes the liberated emissary and partner of Jewish womanism. The prodigal daughter returns to her mother's household.

Overall, the hope of the Jewish-Christian dialogue is seen to be contingent upon its transfiguration into a Jewish-Christian-womanist trialogue.

PART IV

◆

Searchable Judgments

8

♦

Along the Road
of Good Intentions

We have been feeling the pulse of contemporary Jewishness and Christianness in their relations with each other, prevailingly in a North American frame of reference.

The critical assessments contained in Parts II and III of this study are in great measure representational. Many advocates have been heard from: Christian judges of Jewishness, Jewish judges of Christianness, Jewish critics of Jews and Judaism, Christian critics of Christians and Christianity. In the two chapters of this fourth and final part the assessments are much more mine than anyone else's. However, my point of view adopts as its own the hope for the Jewish-Christian meeting expressed at the end of chapter seven: a transfiguration into a Jewish-Christian-feminist meeting. In keeping with this expansion and with one dominant (though not unshared) theme of the women's movement, I suggest that belief-systems are ever subject to judgment at the hands of their human consequences.

No valuation can be absolute. It is subject in turn to evaluation. As against the "unsearchable judgments of God" (Rom 11:33)—themselves sometimes judged yet only by human beings who are pitifully fallible and who do not in fact penetrate the divine unsearchability—human judgments are always searchable. Hence the title of Part IV of this book. Like the claims they assess, the judgments to be made in this chapter and the concluding one—ventured by a solitary Christian—are fragmentary, limited, and, most of all, accountable.

Building upon Samuel Johnson and others, Karl Marx offered the opinion that "the road to hell is paved with good intentions." This finding is not wholly condemnatory. Neither does it annul all hope. For perhaps the traveler can turn off the road onto another before it is too late.

Allusion will be made to five instances of Christian hermeneutic that embody good intentions respecting the Jewish people and Judaism. Praise is due one or another of these protagonists for the zeal with which they oppose the "teaching of contempt." Should they be successful, they will have forsaken the pavement to hell and be on their way to a more blessed destination. But are they going to succeed?

Model one: A splitting of truth

Upon confessedly personalist and interpersonalist grounds, Joseph E. Monti seeks to show the way to a valid Christology for Christians within a frame of reference of the Jewish-Christian encounter. The subtitle of his book *Who Do You Say That I Am?* reflects his recognition of the problem in all its graveness: *The Christian Understanding of Christ and Antisemitism.*

Monti calls upon Christians to have fidelity to *truthful experiences*. On the one hand, he at times maintains that such experiences have meaning only "for us," i.e., for him and other Christians—for which perhaps the analogy may be introduced of monogamous human wedlock, wherein truth and fidelity extend to the partners alone. The trouble is that this emphasis contradicts the traditional Christological claim that Jesus Christ is at once, and objectively, human and divine. Monti fervently retains and preaches this latter claim in other pages. Accordingly, he at times intends "truthful experiences" to have meaning and applicability not alone for him and other Christians, but for all human persons. As he concludes, what Christians experience "is not our own special truth 'just for us' among which there are many others, but *the one truth*—the one and only God of and for all, the one and only Christ, Lord and Savior of and for all." This must only compel him into a conversionist stance toward Jews, subverting his own insistence that Christianity, if it is going to be faithful and moral, must not negate Judaism.[1]

Monti attempts to comprehend Christianity's claims of exclusivity and singularity as an inevitable accompaniment of its monotheism. This is not accurate. In truth, it is the *trinitarianism* of Christianity that has produced those claims. As we have seen, Judaism, which is as monotheist as, or more rigorously monotheist than, Christianity, refuses to make the exclusivist claims that the church makes.

The unresolved difficulty for Monti is metaphysical and epistemological: What is the nature and meaning of truth? His effort to deny "logical exclusivity" to Christianity while insisting upon its "phenomenological identity" fails to meet this question. The question is one of truth as such—substantive truth—and accordingly that question is simply not faced when recourse is had, as in Monti's case, to allegedly different kinds of truth. To illustrate, the eminently simple proposition from the Johannine Jesus, "no one comes to the Father, but by me" (John 14:6), wholly transcends and bridges any advocated division among "truthful experiences," "logical exclusivity," and "phenomenological identity," and it does this in the late twentieth century as much as in the first century. Due to the very character of the language of John 14:6, the proposition is either true or it is false. We are not afforded, alas, any third alternative.

Monti involves himself in the same philosophic difficulty of truth-splitting that suffuses H. Richard Niebuhr's disjunction between "internal history" and "external history,"[2] a severance Monti applauds. In actuality, there is no way to reduce such an event as the Resurrection of Jesus to an "event" of "internal history"—not without completely negating it. Nor is there any way to take the confession, "There is one God in Christ of and for all, there is no other," and to put it, as Monti tries to do, into the category of "internal history," i.e., existential history. Such an effort is self-refuting. The incoherence could be removed only were the statement changed to read, "For us, there is one God in Christ and no other." The words "of and for all" would have to go out. Theological and moral consistency and coherence, when grounded in authentic "phenomenological identity," demand silence or at least agnosticism upon the status of "all people."

Monti's problem is a familiar one in the recent story of Christians vis-à-vis Jews, viz., his intentions are the most praiseworthy yet he does not implement them. The difficulty is that, with many others, he is striving to have things two ways: to be fair and just to Jews while retaining a theological position that has, historically, caused all the unfairness and all the injustice.

Model two: Human unity become enmity

If Joseph E. Monti's problem centers within the nature of truth, the viewpoint of Ronald Goetz, while enmeshed in that difficulty too, drives us much deeper into the way in which universalist, good intentions may be invaded by demonic structures.

In an Easter meditation titled "A Lived Resurrection," Goetz testifies that the Cross and the Resurrection "constitute a powerful vindication from God's side that his saving intention appears limitless." Goetz continues:

> Good Friday and Easter ought not only to be days in which we Christians celebrate God's gift for *our* salvation; they ought also to be days in which the church rejoices in the universal brotherhood and sisterhood of humankind. For what is it that finally unites our apparently polarized and radically pluralistic species? We are divided by sex, race, religion, national origin, ideology, talent, career, personality, size and strength—name an attribute, and it distinguishes each individual from millions or billions of other individuals. However, what unites all, despite the diversity, is Christ's dying for us *all*, and being resurrected as the first fruits of the promise of the eternal life of *all*.
>
> We might go as far as to say that the death and resurrection of Jesus Christ is basic to a true definition of humanity.

A first alert is sounded by the last words here. They quite obviously insinuate that something inhuman appears in any denial of the meaning and truth of Jesus Christ's death and Resurrection. Thus, at the very outset Goetz is building the eventuality of antisemitism into his universalism. However, and significantly, he quickly grants that among the elements of reality that seem "to mock Christian universalism" is nothing other than antisemitism. (Remember, we are reckoning with *good intentions*.) Goetz readily concedes that "human beings often do not take kindly to being 'understood' better than they understand themselves." Yet he then proceeds to reject his own admission:

> The sorry record of Christian anti-Semitism is to some but the bitter fruit of Christian "universalism." It has been argued that only because Christians affirm such things as Christ's divinity and his saving death and resurrection have they presumed to persecute Jews for their "unbelief." The Jews become an affront to Christian universalism's imperialistic implications.
>
> But to demand, as do some Christian theologians, that Christianity, in response to anti-Semitism, give up its claim to Christ's divinity is possible only for those whose understanding of Jesus Christ permits such a unitarian version of the faith. It can be argued that anti-Semitism is being used as a pawn in an essentially theological argument; e.g., "orthodox Christianity has been guilty of anti-Semitism, therefore fair-minded people must

embrace *my* theological alternative." . . . [Round] and round we go: for one person, belief in Christ's divinity jeopardizes the Jews; for another, Christ's divinity so unifies the human race that anti-Semitism—indeed, all bigotry—is blasphemy.[3]

The state of affairs Goetz describes does not prevent him from choosing to ride one horse and none other on the merry-go-round, for in the initial passage cited he has already given us his own certain view. His apostleship is in behalf of the unity of all humankind that is *only* made possible by the death and Resurrection of a divine Jesus Christ. It is this latter persuasion that induces several comments.

(i) It is historically and factually incorrect to pretend that Christ's divinity so unifies the human race that it is able to put antisemitism to shame. The last thing a problem is eligible for is to be identified as a solution. There is as much, or more, evidence for concluding that the reputed divinity of Christ divides the human race and foments antisemitism. Goetz challenges his readers to "name attributes" that separate rather than unite human beings. Here is one that he, unforgivably, rules out: "Christian," contra "non-Christian."

(ii) From Goetz's meditation in its entirety, it is clear that he is striving to maneuver traditionalist Christian faith into a place where it is beyond possible condemnation for failing the test of human consequences, a test proposed at the start of this chapter. Curiously, Goetz suddenly deserts the very theological challenge he is himself bringing. He does this by shifting to the entirely different and non-relevant rubric of demands upon church people to *be* Christian in their conduct. The determining issue of universal truth-claims is hardly resolved through taking refuge in the standards of simple morality, however attractive these are. The utterly grave question, which Goetz blatantly abandons, is how Christians can ever be "little Christs" to their neighbors when they are all the time building an impenetrable barrier to their neighbors through decreeing publicly and absolutely that human unity is possible *only* in and through Jesus Christ.

(iii) Goetz's charge of "unitarianism" as the assumption behind the struggle of some Christian theologians against antisemitism is as patronizing as it is false. What he clearly cannot allow is a totally different motivation: that the inhuman consequences of the imperialist-universalist claims of Christianity have so *revolted* these Christian theologians that they are left with no choice but to demand a radical revision in all Christian belief. If in fact antisemitism is being used today as a "pawn" in a theological argument, this may be more accurately exemplified in Goetz's conversation with himself than anywhere else. The nausea that afflicts his opponents day and night is a moral universe away from all theological gamesmanship.

(iv) The most devastating consideration is that Goetz's claim for the Christian reduces Jews (and, by implication, human beings everywhere) to objects, to non-persons. Thereby does he recapitulate nineteen hundred years of Christian history.

Let us approach the scene from the standpoint of the Jewish people, for this is the one way, in the present frame of reference, that we can ensure the perspective of persons, of subjects, in contrast to objects.

Ronald Goetz is very close to Karl Rahner's viewpoint.[4] Rahner endeavors to make nonbelieving people into "anonymous Christians." In the instance of Goetz, Jews gain their inviolable human dignity only through being anonymous benefactors of Christ's self-sacrifice and love. In Rahner, as in Goetz, Christian arrogance can hardly descend to greater depths—a condition that would be simply impossible were the advocates not operating in the name of opposition to arrogance, i.e., from the very noblest of intentions.

Whenever, as in Goetz's case, Jesus Christ is perceived as the hidden one without whose graceful presence Jews and all humanity would fail to possess dignity, Jews say No to the "gift." Why is that? Are they being perverse? Inhuman? No, the refusal is bonded to an experiential history almost two thousand years long. Jews have learned very well how to recognize a universalism that is false. They can smell it from a thousand miles away. Reflexively, the Jewish people are nay-sayers to sacrilege, to idolatry. Professor Goetz is trying to tell them, in effect, and with the noblest of purposes: "Your very wellbeing in this world is made possible by Jesus Christ, quite apart from whether you are aware of it. Secretly, your existence and your dignity testify to this truth of God. You are really on *my* side, though you do not know it. Your very life, the very potentiality of your life, testifies that, hiddenly, *something has happened in the history of the human world that puts you in agreement with me.*"

The historic Jewish reply is an uncomplicated, human one: "We heard all that from the Inquisition a long time ago. The inquisitors always assured us that they only had our wellbeing at heart. And we have been prepared to go to the stake rather than become the non-persons that they and you have invented." When faced with a choice between Christ as reputed divine dignifier of humankind and the act of martyrdom, very many Jews have chosen martyrdom. Jewish allegiance, conscious or unconscious, is to the Sovereign of the universe. This is how so many Jews have been willing to die rather than surrender to an imperialism that dresses itself in the cloak of anti-imperialism, a triumphalism that masquerades as anti-triumphalism. *Jews know that a human idol dignifies nothing. An idol only destroys human beings.* Jews are with Jesus of Nazareth.

A blasphemy worse than antisemitism is the endeavor to subject Jews to a Christian rendering of all events, to put the entire existential fate and destiny of the Jewish people under the sway of the Christian dispensation. Jews have been certain for a very long time that the real and only reason bigotry is blasphemous is its affront to human beings who are created in the image of God, a certainty in direct opposition to a much later and Christianly-contrived argument for the "truth" of the Christian claim. The definition of Christian triumphalism is: a religious act that transubstantiates human subjects into less-than-human objects.

Thus does the Jewish refutation of the kind of contemporary Christianity typified in Ronald Goetz become identical with the Jewish victory over the *Shoah*: "I will not give you my soul. It is mine, it is God's, it is not yours." We are further reminded here of the moral and universalist superiority of American religious pluralism—for all its limitations—to traditionalist Christian faith: Human beings must be accepted as human beings, with any and all ideological holds barred. In this, the American system is much closer to historic Judaism than to historic Christianity.

(v) The fundamentalist-evangelical demand, "Believe in Jesus or be damned," reflects a moral condition somewhat less objectionable than Goetz's inadvertently anti-Jewish universalism, simply because that other demand is wholly straightforward and wholly transparent. It is entirely possible that Goetz does not actually realize the import of what he is saying, for his intentions are after all the most honorable. His moral qualifications are impeccable. His dedication is to love, to reconciliation, to human unity. The last thing he would consciously wish is the damnation of a single soul. Yet once all this is allowed for, he is nevertheless *acting* decisively and concretely to disarm his opposition with the aid of a crippling deed of *parti pris*, a gargantuan exercise in question-begging—

all made possible by the moral beauty and power of good intentions. Somewhere the shades of Samuel Johnson and Karl Marx will have got together to drink a toast to so winsome an incarnation of their watchword. For what form of imperialism is more disarming than an imperialism overflowing with goodness?

(vi) Revealingly, Ronald Goetz is allied with Joseph E. Monti in an oblique, and doubtless unintended, misrepresentation of Judaism. As we noted, Monti tries to make Christianity's exclusivity a function of its monotheism, thereby and by association incorrectly subjecting Judaism to a like charge, in view of the latter's rigorous monotheism. Goetz involves himself in a parallel difficulty by alleging that whenever people express their most basic beliefs, especially beliefs that are universalist, they create conflict with other human beings. Surely any such outcome is contingent upon the specific quality of the beliefs, the faith-community out of which they come, and the status that community has in the wider world. The affirmations of a tolerationist Jewish monotheism are quite a different thing from traditional Christian imperialism.

All in all, the human unity preached by Ronald Goetz is in fact human enmity.

Model three: Theologization redivivus

Many of the practitioners of a third model are distinguished for being devoted members of the new movement of Christian reform. They are part of the commotion in the back of the church. The pristine goodness of their intentions derives from their warfare against the long-time, *negativist* Christian theologizing of Jews and Judaism. They wholly oppose the ideology that makes the Jewish people no longer the people of God, that abolishes the covenant with Israel due to Israel's "sin." These reformers testify that the Christian faith is grounded upon, and receives its very meaning and authorization from, Israel as people of God. Accordingly, in place of a theologizing negativism vis-à-vis Jews, these advocates set a wholly *positive* hermeneutic. As one of them expresses it, there must be a wholly supportive "Christian theology of the people Israel."

The difficulty here is two-sided and severe. For one thing, as we have noted all along the line Jewishness is more than the religion of Judaism. A state of affairs could of course be imagined where Jews as a whole are religious and identify themselves as the people of God. The difficulty would then vanish. Unhappily or happily, any such envisagement is pure fantasy. Large numbers of Jews simply do not think of themselves in the above terms. Who, then, are Christians to identify them in that way? Where do Christians get the right to religionize them? At an earlier place the point is made that while the words "unbroken covenant between Israel and her saving God" sound guileless enough, to many nonreligious Jews the sentiment constitutes Christian imperialism and also contributes to Jewish wrongheadedness. At Mainz, Pope John Paul II addressed the Jewish leaders of Germany as representing "the people of God of the old covenant never revoked by God" and as "today's people of the covenant concluded with Moses."[5] Here too, seemingly blessed words have a way of carrying us along the pavement of good intentions toward a woeful destination. That consequence is only underscored in and through the frightful experiences of the Jews of the *Shoah*.

The other side of the difficulty is already implied. As indicated in chapter five, one fundamental prerequisite and mark of responsible dialogue is that the right of self-definition and self-identification belongs exclusively to each partner alone.

For all its good intentions, a positive Christian theologizing of Jews cannot escape imperialism. There can be no "Christian theology of the people Israel." The attempt to construct such a theory is tied, in the view of at least one American theologian, Paul M. van Buren, with an effort to make the Christian church into something peculiarly gentile. This effort acts to bolster a supersessionist Christian ideology according to which "the gentiles" tend to replace "the Jews." (Cf. Acts 28:28: "the salvation of God is sent unto the gentiles.") Two parallel European attempts at a wrongful theologizing of Jews and Judaism (with the finest of intentions) are Franz Mussner, *Tractate on the Jews*, and Clemens Thoma, *A Christian Theology of Judaism*.[6]

Any positive Christian theologizing of Jews fabricates the being of Jewishness from the outside—not unlike the ideology of the "Christian Zionism" that deigns to assimilate the being of the State of Israel to Christian ideas and Christian self-interest. "The only legitimate theology of the people Israel is a Jewish one. If Jews wish to opt for a religious identity, fine—and the same goes for their dereligionization. One way or the other, the determination is exclusively theirs, not that of Christians."[7] In the world after the *Shoah*, Christians in particular are forbidden to identify Jewish identity (just as Jews are, in principle, forbidden to identify Christian identity). The fitting Christian *dialogic* rejoinder to any attempted Christian "theology of Judaism and Jewishness" is: "Judaism and Jewishness are what the Jewish people say they are." Nothing else can be legitimately added.*

Potentially, the consequences of our third model are more deleteriously ironic than those of the first two models already assayed because these consequences arise within the inmost circle of today's Christian reform movement. Involved are Christian thinkers who are dedicated, even to the point of devoting an entire life's work, to rectifying the church's derogation of Judaism and the Jewish people, to repudiating the centuries-old Christian crime. Their intentions are the very best, and accordingly the destructiveness of their wholly unintended imperialisms will be that much more fatal and fateful.

Model four: Contra the counsel of Johann Baptist Metz

Professor Metz has been cited as warning Christians away from any theology that could be the same before and after the Holocaust. In keeping with this counsel, the revolutionary changes that are required of Christian doctrine will make the post-*Shoah* teaching of the church an entirely different thing from its pre-*Shoah* teaching. One conspicuous tragedy within the new Christian reform is that many of those who are demanding a transformation of Christian teaching, urging radical alterations in Christian behavior, and calling for a readiness to learn from dialogue with Jews ofttimes come out propounding the very same dogmas that have been at the root of all the trouble through their perpetuating of anti-Judaism and anti-Jewishness.

For example, John T. Pawlikowski seeks to make the Resurrection derivative of the Incarnation, maintaining that Jesus "had to rise because

---

*The forbidding of Christian attempts to define Jewishness and its meaning in the world extends, of course, to the reality of the State of Israel. The content and purposes of the Jewish-Christian dialogue must be carefully and responsibly distinguished from Israeli–non-Israeli relations. Jews and Christians in dialogue are anything but arbiters of the problems of nation-states. The simplest way to remind ourselves of this fact is to imagine an Israeli Jew seeking to introduce into a dialogue with an American Christian the issue of United States policy in, say, Central America. The Israeli would not do this, or if he did, he would be quite out of order. In the same way, American Christians have no business introducing into the Jewish-Christian dialogue such questions as Israeli policy in the so-called West Bank, the treatment of minorities in Israel, and Israeli government policies on peace and war. John T. Pawlikowski: Please note.

he was who he was," viz., a unique and saving union of humanity and divinity. This argument is fully subject to the radical womanist judgment introduced in the final section of chapter seven: the victimization intrinsic to andric incarnationism. Furthermore, Pawlikowski's emphasis is no less supersessionist than a triumphalist Resurrection. It means replacing and, in effect, condemning the Jewish disallowance that a human being could be divine. This disallowance permeates Pharisee and rabbinic Judaism, indeed all Judaism. Humankind is created in the image *of* God; accordingly, no man or woman can ever be called divine (as Pawlikowski in fact concedes respecting Judaism).[8] David S. Shapiro writes, "Man is not God, he cannot become God," though, to be sure, "his behavior can be Godlike."[9] This last is precisely the meaning of the *imago dei:* the *imago dei* is what makes possible the uniquely human *imitatio dei*.

Model five: Demonry within

"When the unclean spirit has gone out of a man, he passes through waterless places seeking rest; and finding none he says, 'I will return to my house from which I came.' And when he comes he finds it swept and put in order. Then he goes and brings seven other spirits more evil than himself, and they enter and dwell there; and the last state of that man becomes worse than the first" (Luke 11:24–26).

The pavement of good intentions is traveled by Joseph E. Monti, Ronald Goetz, John Paul II, Paul M. van Buren, Franz Mussner, Clemens Thoma, John T. Pawlikowski, but yet also by one whom traditional wording dubs "the present writer." In this way the New Testament scenario that adds up to eight unclean spirits gains fulfillment. There could be a little comfort in the truth that the other seven are "more evil than himself" (the text is definitely Irish here) were it not for the fact that "the last state of the man becomes worse than the first," viz., than when he resolved, with the very finest intentions, to clean out the Christian house by starting another book.

Writers are frequently called to task for arrogance; they are sometimes faulted as well for self-effacement. I have never been able to understand the latter objection—especially not when the writings under scrutiny do not hesitate to lambaste the works and behavior of just about everyone else in sight. Where is the special dispensation that permits an author to exempt himself from criticism? (A single explanation that gives me a little pause rules out self-criticism on the ground that such writers are not really being honest but are trying, deviously, to have roses pinned on them for their humility. But what human being, not excluding a self-critical one, is ever capable of knowing his ultimate motives? It appears to me that a danger equal to the above is that the omission of self-criticism will insinuate a possession of final insights and final answers.)

Earlier I suggested that the potential destructiveness of a renewed Christian theologization of Jews (model three) is, if anything, greater than the destructiveness of models one and two. In the same way, the potential evils in my own good intentions are greater, I fear, than those in model three. (We may leave model four at peace for the present.)

The very affirmation, put forward in chapter five, that Judaism and the Jewish people comprise the integral foundation of Christianity may itself only aggravate Christian supersessionism. Where I live, many houses are being built. The foundations I inspect on my walks in what used to be "the country" exhibit only passing significance. They are unfinished realities, merely waiting to be covered over. What counts is the first and second storey, for there is where life will be lived. I have sometimes spoken of Christians as guests in the house of Israel. But even guests have a way, after a while, of taking over things. True, there has been of late something of a struggle in the church to fight off the Marcionite abolition of the Jewish foundation and substance of Christianity. Yet where is there any real promise that the demons of Christian arrogance will not move back into the house? Where is there a truly effective remedy for Christian ambivalence to Judaism and the Jewish people? For that attitude reaches out to ensnare the Jewishness of the New Testament and of Christianity itself. Such ambivalence is perhaps the most fateful of all the Christian world's creations. Within it there lives the haunting eventuality of a transference from the person of Jesus himself to the sin of antisemitism. What better instrumentality is there for getting back at "this Jew" for all his eschatological imperatives than to shame and ravage his own people?

Will not the hidden impulses that are stirred up and the hostilities induced in some Christian readers by the morally inspired attacks contained in this volume upon the sins of Christians and upon certain Christological claims outweigh any possible "good" that might be done through sanctioning the attacks? Do not such attacks comprise a life-and-death threat to the Christian psyche? Christian history has been a witness ever and again to the special targeting that results from human hostility.

The victimization of Jews is an unceasing thing. Indeed, were it not for "those Jews"—so laments the Christian unconscious—the very "need" for Christian "revisionism" would never have come to beset us. At a number of places in this study reference is made to the two fundamental causes of the Jewish-Christian conflict: negativity toward Jews as Jews, and negativity toward Jews as human beings. These two causes surely become one in the frame of reference here involved.

In a word, the protest of more than one Jew of today is unanswerable (I speak morally, only morally): "After 1900 years, is it not time that you Christians just let us alone? Forget all about those vaunted 'Jewish-Christian dialogues'! Stop producing those well-intentioned books! Stop stirring up the demons! Just let us alone!"*

If it is truly so that the pavement to hell is composed of good intentions, it does not follow that good intentions have to end in hell. For if it is truly so that the wrath of humankind can be used to praise God, and if the same goes for human error, does it not go as well for good intentions? Yet a more grace-full choice, if it is not illusory, is to travel a different road altogether—not, to be sure, a road of bad intentions but one along which human intention may find itself transformed. Is there, anywhere, such a road?

---

*For many years I have questioned my own critical work, wondering whether it will only serve to aggravate antisemitism more than it meliorates it. Of course, I have no proof of any such consequence. Had I been afforded proof, I should long since have ceased operations. People are enabled to keep going only because they are barred from knowing the final effects of what they say and do.

9

◆

Somewhere Another Road

A fundamental moral-theological dilemma of this book does no more than recapitulate a historic dilemma of Christian existence: How are Christians ever to claim participation in an unbroken divine covenant with Israel without at the same time theologizing Jews, without subjecting the Jewish people and Judaism to Christian religious imperialism? Put differently, how is Christian identity to surmount its negation of Jewish identity?

At various way stations along a hoped-for, new and different road some help may be afforded in facing up to this dilemma, though the reflections that close this book will not finally resolve the dilemma. These reflections tend to divide into two kinds: preliminary-critical and more constructive-affirmational.

Preparation

Though such is not their main purpose, the themes to follow will also do a little reviewing for us.

The gateway. On August 1, 1979, an American Christian of German and Irish descent walked through the entrance to Auschwitz. Above him the black metal banner still hung: *Arbeit macht frei,* Work will liberate you. Before him lay the same barracks, the same gas chambers, and the rubble of the crematoria.

Most of those who entered Auschwitz during the *Shoah* departed as smoke in the sky. With his wife and colleagues and friends, this individual was to leave in a gleaming motor coach. I was that person. Therefore, I can make no claims.

State of the siege of Auschwitz. At the conclusion of his study of modern antisemitism, Jacob Katz alludes to the new Christian revisionist effort to fight anti-Jewishness in the Christian church. Professor Katz is doubtful that the movement will succeed, since "such a revision would subvert the whole doctrinal edifice of Christianity." He thinks it probable that "the revisionary trend . . . will remain an esoteric exercise restricted in its impact to an intellectual elite."[1] Katz's prognosis may well prove correct. Yet one positive implication of his judgment stands: The defeat today of traditionalist Christianity would mean a substantial setback for antisemitism.

For Richard L. Rubenstein in *After Auschwitz* as elsewhere, the life of faith meets its nemesis in the Holocaust. Such a finding applies much more to the Christian world than to the Jewish one. There is no way to deny that an end-consequence of the covenant of God and Israel was the *Shoah*. Nevertheless, an inherently Jewish *response* to the Holocaust is still possible. The Jew is yet able to say, as does Martin A. Cohen, that "the full humanization" of the species persists as "the sacred task of the post-Auschwitz Jew."[2] But how can there be any integrally Christian response? For the Christian dispensation was a cause of the *Shoah*. The post-Holocaust fiat of Irving Greenberg, that no statement, theological or other, may be made "that would not be credible in the presence of the burning children,"[3] may surely be directed against elements of the Jewish tradition and against some Jewish thinking of today. Yet, at base, the fiat is indicting Christianity[4]—not alone for its past but also for its present and for its future.

The models we reviewed in chapter eight help to underscore the truth that Christian derogation of Judaism and the Jewish people is not grounded in what Jews do or do not do, nor even in what the church charges them with doing or not doing. Instead, the issue comes to arise from out of Christianity-in-and-of-itself, Christianity taken in a wholly nonrelational and internal way: its Christology and, most gravely, its teaching of an actualized Resurrection. This means that the church's primary problem is not so much one of changing its attitude toward Jews as it is the need for a revolutionary transformation within its own peculiar teaching and praxis.

However, there must be vigilance against the temptation of moralism.

On moralism. Franklin H. Littell refers to the moralism that Reinhold Niebuhr used to deplore. Littell concludes that "moralism consists in presenting ideal proposals as an alternative to real choices."

The crime that lives. Were the crime of Christendom a thing of the past, by now everything could have been changed. The entire moral problem could long since have been disposed of with aid from appropriately effective dosages of the psychologistic medicine familiar to us all:

Never permit obsession with past guilt to control you, for that is foolishly and unwarrantedly destructive, not just for you but as well for all your aggrieved brothers and sisters.

Sadly, none of this applies. The teachings that victimize human beings (cf. the exposition of the Resurrection in chapter five) are promulgated as much today as they ever were. The crime goes on. Christian supersessionism and an imperializing Resurrection continue to serve as the center and climax of church teaching, preaching, and liturgy.

The focal issue for traditionalist Christology, and hence for Christianity as such, is not, in the first instance, intellectual or spiritual unbelievability. The issue is simple immorality, a most concrete species of human victimization and hostility. Essentially, intellectual and spiritual believability is contingent upon a moral factor. Is Christianity morally credible?

The truth in falsification. In chapter four of this book Emil L. Fackenheim is cited respecting a continuing crisis of Judaism: "After Auschwitz, it is a major question whether the Messianic faith is not *already* falsified—whether a Messiah who could come, and yet at Auschwitz did not come, has not become a religious impossibility." The question of whether Judaism is falsifiable by history is strictly the business of Jews, not of Christians. However, Fackenheim's judgment may be adapted to the crisis of late twentieth-century Christianity: After Auschwitz, it is a major question whether the Christian Messianic faith is not falsified— whether Jesus as the Christ has not become a moral and therefore a religious impossibility. The evidence, if evidence is still needed, that the Resurrection of Jesus cannot in fact embody eschatological fulfillment, even a fragmentary realization of such fulfillment, is that event's contribution to the murders of millions of human beings, including great numbers of children. Thus are Christians summoned to grapple with their own shattering questions: Is Christianity immune, or is it not immune, to events since Jesus? Can something unprecedented serve to bring the Christian faith to trial? Is the Christian faith falsifiable by history? These questions merge into another: Does not the God whose holiness is proved by righteousness dwell in the thick of the historic-moral struggle against Christian antisemitism? David Tracy contends that in light of the Holocaust, Christian theologians can and should challenge "even authoritative scriptural interpretations of the event of Jesus Christ (e.g., 'fulfillment' interpretations which do exist after all in the New Testament alongside other more eschatologically 'not yet' interpretations)."[5] Accordingly, it may be suggested that the life of God and the struggle against antisemitism meet and become as one, in ice-hot judgment against any denial that Christianity can be falsified by history.

On revelation. Whether in fact the *Shoah* will ever gain acceptance by Christian theology and the church as "revelatory" and in consequence as religiously revolutionary is an open question. There are mountainous obstacles: unconquered anti-Judaism and antisemitism, the unresolved trauma of the Holocaust for Christians, and the inability or unwillingness among many church people to believe that there can be new revelatory events beyond the Incarnation-Crucifixion-Resurrection. Donald A. Hagner, an evangelical Christian, denies, flat out, that divine revelation is possible beyond the biblical books.[6] When push comes to shove, vast numbers of Christians will go along with him—by no means all of them fundamentalists. Hagner is saying, in effect and perhaps without having thought through any such implication, that the God of ongoing history is dead and the Holy Spirit is out of commission. Is it right to accept these conclusions?

Affirmation

Along a new and different road a section is reached where from time to time actual glimpses of home are caught.

Metanoia. Samuel Sandmel writes: "I do not regard Judaism as objectively superior to Christianity, nor Christianity to Judaism. Rather, Judaism is mine, and I consider it good, and I am at home in it, and I love it, and want it. That is how I want Christians to feel about their Christianity."[7] But for Christians to be enabled to view their faith the way Sandmel views his Judaism, there has to be a transformation of Christianity, because according to the traditionalist Christian vis-à-vis, the Christian faith is superior. It is the judgment and fulfillment of Judaism. Therefore, if Christians are honestly to "consider their faith good," they have to be helped to repudiate these imperialistic notions.

Of some aid in this repudiation is the finding (at once historical, theological, and moral) that the Jewish people live out their faithfulness to God precisely through being other than Christians. As Rosemary Ruether reasons, once Jews are no longer faulted for their nonacceptance of Christ, the entire Christian inheritance-claim upon the Jewish messianic hope is thrown into question. "The connecting thread linking Jewish messianic expectation, Jesus' historical life and acts, and Christianity [is] broken." These things lie "like so many disparate pieces, tendentiously tied together by later Christian mythmaking."[8]

In proof of holiness. Church people within the moral and secular world of today may be asked to make a decision: Was the prophet Isaiah correct or was he mistaken when he declared that God is proved holy by righteousness (Isa. 5:16)? Those Christians who testify that Isaiah was correct will insist that the right combination of ways for the Christian church to show its faithfulness to God today is through unrelenting and revolutionary self-criticism, radical self-reform in the theological domain, and most of all a dedication to human justice.

In the measure that there is Christian agreement with Isaiah, the counsel of Professor Fackenheim that the priority for Christians is theological self-understanding may be given final expression in this form: The discrete intellectual-moral challenge for future Christian thinking has expanded itself into the quadrilemma of how to interrelate responsibly revelation, new and unprecedented events of history, ethics, and Christology. Thus may Christians of today be guided into transforming kinds of theological revision. The question is no mere theoretical one of whether the events of history vindicate faith or refute faith. The summons to Christians—but also to Jews—is a life-and-death one: to become utterly historical human beings when it comes to the ultimate reaches and ostensible resources of faith. This last eventuality need not entail the betrayal of faith, for faith may be raised to the level of courage, "the courage to be,"[9] within the exciting drama of history.

The image of God. According to Rabbi ben Azzai in the Talmud, the human being as created in God's image is the fundamental Jewish value.[10] Christians can be those people who, from just beyond Judaism, are given a chance to make that same value their own. This eventuality may have a threefold consequence, which speaks to the central Christian dilemma that opens this chapter: Jews and Judaism are not being theologized; Christianity is not being reduced to Judaism; and a peculiarly covenantal task for Christians is being pointed up.

The price of unqualified Christian fealty to the *imago dei* may seem astronomical and creative of anguish, and many people may in consequence back completely off. That price is revisionism at the place of the Incarnation. Unqualified fealty to the image of God will replicate the cost of discipleship to Jesus the Jew, God-centered *Stellvertreter* of the people Israel. For, as noted in chapter eight, the biblical teaching of the image of God simply contradicts the teaching of incarnationism. To be *of* God is the opposite of ever *being* God—just as the creation as a whole is *of* God and therefore *not* God. The anti-incarnationist, moral-theological emphasis deriving from the doctrine that humankind is made in the image of God comprises the basis for the reconstruction of a uniquely integral and distinctive Christianity that will have vanquished its Christological idolatries. In the presence of the *imago dei,* incarnationism is revealed in all its falsity. And once the image of God is celebrated in its universal dimension, the *imitatio dei* can go freely to work. (In no way is it implied here that one must be either a Jew or a Christian to be freed of idolatry. Other world faiths are fully part of the creation along with Judaism and Christianity. Their people are blessed with the image of God as much as anyone else.)

Jesus was a specialist in celebrating the image of God. In the Sermon on the Mount all sorts and conditions of people embody that image and are blessed: the poor in spirit, the mourners, the meek, those who covet righteousness, the merciful, the pure in heart, the peacemakers, the persecuted (Matt. 5:3–10). What is left to do is to assemble the pitiable others: the rich in spirit, the merrymakers, the arrogant, those who hunger and thirst for unrighteousness, the unmerciful, the impure in heart, the warmakers, the persecutors—plus the tax collectors, the prostitutes (Matt. 21:31), and the prodigals. Now, finally, the guest list is filled out.

The integrity and the irreplaceableness of Christianity center in Christian people and what they do rather than in an exclusivist dogma. John Hick identifies the peculiarity of Christianity as the response of discipleship to Jesus of Nazareth.[11]

Acceptance. If the traditionalist Christian claim is *not* falsified by history, how is supersessionist anti-Jewishness to be vanquished? But if that claim is *wholly* falsified by history, will this mean that the Christian assurance of God's acceptance of the unacceptable (chapter five, section II [d]) is extinguished? To compress the two sides of the predicament into a single question: How is it possible for there to be Christians who are, at once, unqualifiedly accepting of the Jewish people and themselves unqualifiedly accepted by God? Or does the ultimate existential choice have to be between antisemitism and pagan forlornness?

Let us pursue the dialectic to its denouement, however anguishing that may prove. On the one hand, the Christian crime lives on (thesis). On the other hand, the Christian is said to be accepted (antithesis). Is there, somewhere, a redeeming synthesis?

If the pavement to hell is in fact composed of good intentions, it may be suggested, haltingly yet persevering in the final theme of chapter five, that the way to heaven is paved with acceptance: a divine acceptance of human beings, and a responding acceptance by poor human creatures of other poor human creatures. Yet is it not morally reprehensible to maintain thesis and antithesis together? How can there be genuine acceptance of those who continue in their transgressions? Worse: Is it not objectively wrong to be granted forgiveness while abiding in one's sins? Worse still: Is not God herself/himself a transgressor in accepting, and thereby condoning, evil?

Such questions are as ancient as religion and as humankind.

The formidable danger persists that Christians will keep on theologizing Jews. To make human beings into non-persons is a final evil. One potential resource for countering this state of affairs is *a radical humanization of the covenant*. For a humanizing covenant is not untrue to the traditional faith of Judaism and it is not unfaithful to the wishes of nonreligious Jews. Need it be untrue or unfaithful to the faith of Christianity? Jewish believers and Jewish nonbelievers may be brought together through this very humanization. And so may Christians. And so may Jews and Christians.

The theological-moral question of how the God of Israel may move to accept the unacceptable outsider requires painstaking and delicate exposition. Such exposition lacks systematic treatment in this book, which is not a study in atonement or divine-human reconciliation or constructive (as against critical) Christology.[12] However, one potential resource for the Christian has been hiding itself within these pages. That resource is constituent to the essay as a whole. We return to it for a last time: the State of Israel.

The other side of a reputed Christian victory through the Resurrection is the reputed defeat of the "old Israel," as manifest in wandering Jews barred from the Land because of their sins. But since 1948 the Third Jewish Commonwealth has lived. What is going on there? Could it be that some kind of divine comedy is being staged? The event of Israel is of benefit to many, most of all to the Jewish people. May it also bring a message for the Christian world?

The Christian who turns from a traditionalist life (or faith) of crime may find himself or herself driven to a most terrible eventuality: the aloneness of no longer being accepted. *For is it not through the Resurrection of Jesus Christ that the aloneness of those beyond the original covenant is supposed to be resolved?* "If Christ has not been raised, your faith is futile" (I Cor. 15:17). Thus, in the last resort, i.e., in the final extremity of life, the question presents itself: Is the ancient God of Israel a defeated God? Has this God grown old and impotent? Is this God now bereft of resources, of redeeming power? If so, Christian forlornness is matched by the forlornness of God. And the end has to be the end of human hope.

As the catastrophic twentieth century draws near its end, the question to the Christian community is whether there is a historical word from God that will at once deliver the Christian church from forlornness and deliver it from its unabated victimization of the Jewish people. Is there somewhere a special historical event that judges and redeems the victimizing Resurrection? Is there somewhere an event of God that in the very moment Christians are assailed by the moral trauma of necessarily rejecting the Resurrection in its victimizing aspects, will nevertheless bring assurance, an event that will say "I accept you"?

Such an event may be the State of Israel as a contemporaneous act, a sign, from the God of Israel. This is not to imply that Christians are in any way privy to that event. Israel remains the property of the Jewish people. By no means has the danger been lifted that Christians will just perdure in their habit (not unlike a collective drug habit) of treating Jews as a means to a Christian end—as in the ideology of "Christian Zionism." But the contention here is a universe removed from "Christian Zionism." The one allowable gift for Christians is the State of Israel as a historical witness that God continues to accept human beings wholly *apart from* the Resurrection of Jesus Christ. It is exactly here, Robert A. Everett proposes, that the Israel of today may be received as sacramental for Christians. Israel is saying to Christians: Your victimization of Jews and Judaism is in no way a function of your human acceptance by God and hence it is not necessary to your acceptance of *yourself*. You simply do not need any such "works-righteousness"—or "works-unrighteousness." *You do not even have to be "religious."* You are given a new chance now to live wholly by grace. And, therefore, the Christian response to this gift, a special way for Christians to show their thanksgiving, is their faithful support of the State of Israel.

Thus may the Christian crime against Jews be obviated and Christian people saved from forlornness. The State of Israel may be construed as a liberating, divine-historical event, which, in addition to being an end in itself for the sake of the Jewish people and human freedom everywhere, acts to heal the history that has profaned the Resurrection of Jesus into a weapon of victimization. (The challenge to propound a non-eschatological, non-triumphalist teaching of the Resurrection is here left open, and with it the winsome possibility that the Resurrection may still find a place in Christian teaching.) Two events, the Resurrection of Jesus and the restoration of the State of Israel, are linked, astonishingly yet indissolubly, the one in its destructiveness, the other as judge and redeemer of that destructiveness. In principle, the causal place of the Resurrection, and hence of Christianity in its entirety, in the Abomination against the Jewish people is annulled. And the Christian faith is made whole. It is restored to its integrity. Peace is brought between the thesis of criminality and the antithesis of acceptance. A strange synthesis is made manifest, and it is not an idea. It is a deed.

The children. In the last reckoning, it is not through thought or theology and perhaps not even through religious faith that we are brought to look into the faces and to hear the cries of the distraught children. We honor and remember them best whenever we act to keep safe the little ones of today and tomorrow. On that note this story for the sake of the children is ended.

NOTES

Abbreviations

CC   *The Christian Century*
FF   *Face to Face*
MID *Midstream*
NYT *The New York Times*
PT   *Present Tense*

Where a source is cited a first time without complete bibliographical information, the full citation is found in the bibliography below.

1. Two Identities

1. See article "Christianity," *Encyclopaedia Judaica* 5: 507.
2. Lawrence J. Silberstein, "Judaism as a Secular System of Meaning: The Writings of Aḥad Haam," *Journal of the American Academy of Religion* 42 (1984): 548.
3. Stuart E. Rosenberg, *The New Jewish Identity in America*, xiii.

2. The Inveterate Vis-à-Vis

1. Donald A. Hagner, *The Jewish Reclamation of Jesus: An Analysis and Critique of Modern Jewish Study of Jesus* (Grand Rapids: Academie Books–Zondervan, 1984), 16.
2. See Uriel Tal, "Structures of Fellowship and Community in Judaism," *Conservative Judaism* 28 (1974): 4.
3. John T. Pawlikowski, *What Are They Saying About Christian-Jewish Relations?*, 99; cf. Pawlikowski, *Christ in the Light of the Christian-Jewish Dialogue*, chap. 4; Philip Culbertson, "The Pharisaic Jesus and His Gospel Parables," *CC* 102 (1985): 74–77.
4. Consult Edward Schillebeeckx, *Jesus: An Experiment in Christology*, trans. Hubert Hoskins (New York: Seabury, 1979); Hyam Maccoby, *Revolution in Judaea: Jesus and the Jewish Resistance* (New York: Taplinger, 1973); and John T. Townsend, "Israel's Land Promises Under the New Covenant," unpublished paper for the Israel Study Group, 1972.
5. Martin Buber, *Israel and the World: Essays in a Time of Crisis*, 2nd ed. (New York: Schocken Books, 1963), 36.
6. Gregory Baum, Introduction to Rosemary Radford Ruether, *Faith and Fratricide*, 6. See also E. P. Sanders, *Paul, the Law, and the Jewish People*.

7. John Frederick Jansen, *The Resurrection of Jesus Christ in New Testament Theology*, 22, 84–85, 89, 92, 91.

8. Carroll E. Simcox, "Communion and Communication," *CC* 101 (1984): 895, 896.

9. Franz Rosenzweig, as cited in Walter Jacob, *Christianity Through Jewish Eyes*, 124.

10. "Christianity," *Encyclopaedia Judaica* 5: 507.

11. Haim Cohn, *The Trial and Death of Jesus* (New York: Harper & Row, 1971), 331.

12. "Statement on Catholic-Jewish Relations," U.S. National Conference of Catholic Bishops, November 1975, in Helga Croner, compiler, *Stepping Stones to Further Jewish-Christian Relations*, 32.

13. Jacob, *Christianity Through Jewish Eyes*, 11.

14. Moses Maimonides, *Mishneh Torah, Hilkhot Melakhim*, XI:4, as cited (with minor emendation) in Jacob, *Christianity Through Jewish Eyes*, 11.

15. Philip Hallie, *Lest Innocent Blood Be Shed* (New York: Harper & Row, 1979).

16. Peter Grose, *Israel in the Mind of America*, 316.

17. David S. Wyman, *The Abandonment of the Jews: America and the Holocaust, 1941–1945* (New York: Pantheon Books, 1984); cf. Grose, *Israel in the Mind of America*.

18. Eugene B. Borowitz, *Contemporary Christologies*, 33.

3. The Abomination

1. Arthur A. Cohen, *The Tremendum*.

2. Yosef Hayim Yerushalmi, "Response to Rosemary Ruether," in Eva Fleischner, ed., *Auschwitz*, 103.

3. Ibid.

4. Emil L. Fackenheim, *The Jewish Return Into History: Reflections in the Age of Auschwitz and a New Jerusalem* (New York: Schocken Books, 1978), 76.

5. Emil L. Fackenheim, *To Mend the World*, 28.

6. Ibid., 12.

7. Primo Levi, *Survival in Auschwitz*, trans. Stuart Woolf (New York: Orion, 1959), 82.

8. Fackenheim, *To Mend the World*, 282–283.

9. Emil L. Fackenheim, unpublished paper "The Holocaust: A Summing Up After Two Decades of Reflection" (1984). Consult as well the essay "The 'Unique' Intentionality of the Holocaust" by Steven T. Katz, in his work *Post-Holocaust Dialogues: Critical Studies in Modern Jewish Thought* (New York: New York University Press, 1983); also Cohen, *The Tremendum*.

10. Fackenheim, *To Mend the World*, 206–215; Terence Des Pres, *The Survivor: An Anatomy of Life in the Death Camps* (New York: Oxford University Press, 1976), chap. 3, "Excremental Assault."

11. See Fackenheim, "Resistance as an Ontological Category," in *To Mend the World*, 225–250.

12. Fackenheim, *To Mend the World*, pp. 12–13.

13. Elie Wiesel, "A Personal Response," *FF* 6 (1979): 37.

14. Robert McAfee Brown, *Elie Wiesel*, 171.

15. Fackenheim, *To Mend the World*, 284.

16. Fackenheim, "Holocaust."

4. The New Jewish Stand

1. Martin E. Marty, "Peace and Pluralism: The Century 1946–1952," *CC* 101 (1984): 979.

2. Robert T. Handy, *A Christian America: Protestant Hopes and Historical Realities* (New York: Oxford University Press, 1971), 213.

3. A. James Rudin, *Israel for Christians*, 12, 17.

4. Pinchas Peli, as cited by Alice L. Eckardt, "Power and Powerlessness: The Jewish Experience," in Israel W. Charny, ed., *Toward the Understanding and Prevention of Genocide*, Proceedings of the International Conference on the Holocaust and Genocide (Boulder/London: Westview, 1984), 195.

5. Alice L. Eckardt, "Power and Powerlessness," 193; Yehuda Bauer, *The Jewish Emergence from Powerlessness*.

6. Bauer, *Jewish Emergence from Powerlessness*.

7. Livia Bitton-Jackson, *Madonna or Courtesan? The Jewish Woman in Christian Literature* (New York: Seabury, 1982), 119.

8. See Rudin, *Israel for Christians*, 24–25; in general, chap. 2, "The Rise of Modern Zionism."

9. Stuart E. Rosenberg, *The New Jewish Identity in America*, 69.

10. W. D. Davies, "Introductory Reflections," Symposium on "The Territorial Dimension of Judaism," *MID* 29 (1983): 32.

11. John T. Pawlikowski, *What Are They Saying About Christian-Jewish Relations?*, 113–114.

12. Alice L. Eckardt, "Power and Powerlessness," 191, 193.

13. Arnold M. Eisen, *The Chosen People in America*.

14. Jonathan D. Sarna, "The Great American Jewish Awakening," *MID* 28 (1982): 33.

15. Eisen, *Chosen People in America*, 144–147, 167–170.

16. Ibid., chaps. 1, 6, 7.

17. Rosenberg, *New Jewish Identity in America*, 64, 65.

18. Ibid., 211–212.

19. Ibid., 213–214.

20. Robert M. Seltzer, *Jewish People, Jewish Thought*, 683; Rosenberg, *New Jewish Identity in America*, 78.

21. Rosenberg, *New Jewish Identity in America*, 130.

22. "What It Means," editorial in *Near East Report* 28 (1984): 185.

23. Rosenberg, *New Jewish Identity in America*, 74.

24. Ibid., 85, 73, 86, 132.

25. Seltzer, *Jewish People, Jewish Thought*, 760.

26. Nathan Perlmutter and Ruth Ann Perlmutter, *The Real Anti-Semitism in America*, 282.

27. A *New York Times* exit poll found that fairness to the poor influenced 25 percent of the Jewish vote, but only 18, 14, and 15 percent, respectively, of the white Catholic, white "born-again" Protestant, and other white Protestant vote. And Jews were noticeably less concerned than the three other groups over the economy and the federal deficit (*NYT*, Nov. 25, 1984).

28. TRB, in the *New Republic*, Dec. 3, 1984, as cited in *Near East Report* 28 (1984): 196.

29. Will Herberg, "The Integration of the Jew in Contemporary America," *Conservative Judaism* 15 (1961): 9.

30. Rosenberg, *New Jewish Identity in America*, 189.

31. Paul Tillich, "Freedom and Ultimate Concern" in John Cogley, ed., *Religion in America* (New York: Meridian, 1958), 282.

32. Eliezer Berkovits, "The Hiding God of History," in Yisrael Gutman and Livia Rothkirchen, eds., *The Catastrophe of European Jewry: Antecedents-History-Reflections* (Jerusalem: Yad Vashem, 1976), 704.

33. Elie Wiesel, *The Trial of God*, a play, trans. Marion Wiesel (New York: Random House, 1979).

34. Michael Chernick, unpublished commentary upon Job 13:15 (Chernick trans.).

35. Elie Wiesel, *A Beggar in Jerusalem*, trans. Lily Edelman and Elie Wiesel (New York: Random House, 1970), 117.

36. James M. Gustafson, *Ethics From A Theocentric Perspective*, Vol. I, 343.

37. Consult, among his other works, Richard L. Rubenstein, *After Auschwitz: Radical Theology and Contemporary Judaism* (Indianapolis: Bobbs-Merrill, 1966).

38. Rubenstein, *After Auschwitz*, 68, 119.

39. Emil L. Fackenheim, *The Jewish Return Into History* (New York: Schocken Books, 1978), part two and esp. chap. 2.

40. Ibid., 44.

41. Emil L. Fackenheim, *Encounters Between Judaism and Modern Philosophy: A Preface to Future Jewish Thought* (New York: Basic Books, 1973), 20–21.

42. Emil L. Fackenheim, *To Mend the World*, 13.

43. Ibid., 311, 300, 301.

44. Ibid., 312.

45. Steven T. Katz, *Post-Holocaust Dialogues* (New York: New York University Press, 1983), 154.

46. Irving Greenberg, "Cloud of Smoke, Pillar of Fire: Judaism, Christianity, and Modernity after the Holocaust," in Eva Fleischner, ed., *Auschwitz*, 11.

47. Ibid., 27–29, 33.

48. A. Roy Eckardt and Alice L. Eckardt, *Long Night's Journey Into Day*, 79–80; Irving Greenberg, *Voluntary Covenant*.

49. See Irving Greenberg, *The Third Great Cycle in Jewish History; On the Third Era in Jewish History: Power and Politics* (New York: National Jewish Resource Center, 1980).

50. Irving Greenberg, "A Broken (Heart/Faith/Love) Is Stronger," *Perspectives*, National Jewish Resource Center, 1983.

51. Eugene B. Borowitz, "On the Jewish Obsession with History," in Leroy S. Rouner, ed., *Religious Pluralism*, 20.

52. Consult article "Resurrection" in *Encyclopaedia Judaica*.

53. Greenberg, "Cloud of Smoke," 30.

54. Abraham J. Heschel, *The Prophets*, Vol. I (New York: Harper & Row, 1962), 113.

55. Helga Croner and Leon Klenicki, eds., *Issues in the Jewish-Christian Dialogue*, part two.

56. Daniel Polish, "Witnessing God after Auschwitz," ibid., 135.

57. Martin A. Cohen, "The Mission of Israel after Auschwitz," ibid., 165.

58. Ibid., 161.

59. Ben Zion Bokser, "Witness and Mission in Judaism," in Croner and Klenicki, eds., *Issues in the Jewish-Christian Dialogue*, 89, 93, 95.

60. Arthur Hertzberg, "The Present Position of Jews in America," *Christianity and Crisis* 43 (1983): 60.

61. Rosenberg, *New Jewish Identity in America*, 132, 268.

62. Cohen, "Mission of Israel," 164, 169.

63. Bokser, "Witness and Mission in Judaism," 102.

64. Rosenberg, *New Jewish Identity in America*, 269, 133.

65. Irving Greenberg, "The '80s: A Time for Nuts and Bolts," *Perspectives*, National Jewish Resource Center, November 1984, 4.

66. Arthur A. Cohen, "Embarrassed by Principle" (part of a symposium), *PT* 12 (1985): 42.

67. Donald A. Hagner, *The Jewish Reclamation of Jesus* (Grand Rapids: Academie Books–Zondervan, 1984), 22, 281–282, 284.

68. Consult Pinchas Lapide, *Israelis, Jews, and Jesus;* cf. Trude Weiss-Rosmarin, ed., *Jewish Expressions on Jesus*.

5. Commotion in the Back of the Church

1. Rosemary Radford Ruether, *Faith and Fratricide*.

2. Monika Hellwig, "Legitimate Complementarity," *FF* 11 (1984): 15–17.

3. David Tracy, "Religious Values After the Holocaust: A Catholic View," in Abraham J. Peck, ed., *Jews and Christians After the Holocaust*, 94.

4. Raymond E. Brown, as cited in Eugene J. Fisher, "The Impact of the Christian-Jewish Dialogue on Biblical Studies," in Richard W. Rousseau, ed., *Christianity and Judaism*, 137–138.

5. Robert L. Brashear, "Corner-Stone, Stumbling-Stone: Christian Problems in Viewing Israel," *Union Seminary Quarterly Review* 38 (1983): 209–210.

6. Ruth Kastning-Olmesdahl, "Theological and Psychological Barriers to Changing the Image of Jews and Judaism in Education," *Journal of Ecumenical Studies* 21 (1984): 468.

7. Franklin H. Littell, "Teaching the Holocaust and Its Lessons" (editorial), *Journal of Ecumenical Studies* 21 (1984): 535.

8. Johann Baptist Metz, in G. B. Ginzel, ed., *Auschwitz als Herausforderung für Juden und Christen* (Heidelberg: Verlag Lambert Schneider, 1980), 176.

9. Harold H. Ditmanson, "Some Theological Perspectives," *FF* 3–4 (1977): 8.

10. Elie Wiesel, *A Jew Today,* trans. Marion Wiesel (New York: Random House, 1978), 13.

11. Daniel F. Polish, "Contemporary Jewish Attitudes to Mission and Conversion," in Martin A. Cohen and Helga Croner, eds., *Christian Mission/Jewish Mission,* 165, 160, 164.

12. Carl F. H. Henry, "Christian Mission Must Continue," *FF* 3–4 (1977): 17.

13. Robert E. Willis, "Auschwitz and the Nurturing of Conscience," *Religion in Life* 44 (1975): 438.

14. Emil L. Fackenheim, unpublished paper, "The Holocaust."

15. Henry, "Christian Mission Must Continue," 17.

16. Ditmanson, "Some Theological Perspectives," 8; Hellwig, "Legitimate Complementarity."

17. Alice L. Eckardt, "The Enigma of Christian Hostility to Israel," *Women's League Outlook* 62 (1972): 25.

18. On the latter element, consult Lawrence J. Epstein, *Zion's Call: Christian Contributions to the Origins and Development of Israel* (Lanham, Md.: University Press of America, 1984).

19. Consult A. Roy and Alice L. Eckardt, "Again, Silence in the Churches," *CC* 84 (1967): 970–973; 992–995.

20. See, e.g., Hertzel Fishman, *American Protestantism and the Jewish State* (Detroit: Wayne State University Press, 1973); Esther Yolles Feldblum, *The American Catholic Press and the Jewish State 1917–1959* (New York: Ktav, 1977).

21. Martin E. Marty, "War's Dilemmas: The Century 1938–1945," *CC* 101 (1984): 868; "Peace and Pluralism," 981.

22. James M. Wall, "Adopting Realism: The Century 1962–1971," *CC* 101 (1984): 1170–1173.

23. *NYT,* May 8, 1972.

24. Hans Küng, in Hans Küng and Walter Kasper, eds., *Christians and Jews* (New York: Seabury, 1975), 11.

25. *Current Dialogue* (Geneva: World Council of Churches), No. 2 (1981): 5–11; No. 4 (1982–83): 5–12.

26. J. A. Emerson Vermaat, "The World Council of Churches, Israel, and the PLO," *MID* 30 (1984): 3–9.

27. Judith Banki, *Anti-Israel Influences in American Churches* (New York: American Jewish Committee, 1980); Brashear, "Corner-Stone, Stumbling-Stone"; "Church Council Scored in Stand," *NYT,* Oct. 16, 1973; A. Roy Eckardt, "The Devil and Yom Kippur," *MID* 20 (1974): 67–75; idem, *Your People, My People: The Meeting of Jews and Christians* (New York: Quadrangle/New York Times, 1974), 128–135; Epstein, *Zion's Call,* p. 127; "Message From the Consultation on Christian Presence and Witness in the Middle East," Geneva, May 15–19, 1983, Middle East Council of Churches and WCC, *Current Dialogue* (Geneva: WCC), No. 5 (1983): 27–29; Nathan Perlmutter and Ruth Ann Perlmutter, *The Real Anti-Semitism in America,* chap. 7; "Statement on the Middle East," Sixth Assembly, World Council of Churches, Vancouver, July 24–Aug. 10, 1983, *Current Dialogue,* No. 6 (1984): 16–17; Vermaat, "World Council of Churches."

28. This point of view is described in A. Roy Eckardt, "Theological Implications of the State of Israel: The Protestant View," *Encyclopaedia Judaica Year Book* 1974, 158–159.

29. *The Diaries of Theodor Herzl*, trans. and ed. Marvin Lowenthal (New York: Grosset & Dunlap, 1962), 428, 429.

30. A. Roy Eckardt, "Theological Implications," 161.

31. We are reminded here of those Christian fundamentalists who profess fervent religious support for the Jewish state but who also back politicians who oppose American aid to Israel. Sol Stern, "The Falwell Fallacy: The Limits of Fundamentalist Support for Israel," *Reform Judaism* (Winter 1984–1985), 5–6. On Jerry Falwell's position on the State of Israel, consult Merrill Simon, *Jerry Falwell and the Jews* (New York: Jonathan David, 1984); Epstein, *Zion's Call*, 130–132.

32. A. Roy Eckardt, "Theological Implications," 162.

33. Ibid., 163.

34. James Parkes, *Whose Land?* 136.

35. Pope John Paul II, as cited by Leon Klenicki, "Basic Jewish and Christian Beliefs in Dialogue," *Pace* 13 (1982): 2, italics added.

36. Joan Peters, *From Time Immemorial: The Origins of the Arab-Jewish Conflict over Palestine* (New York: Harper & Row, 1984).

37. Emil L. Fackenheim, *To Mend the World*, 14.

38. Ruether, *Faith and Fratricide*, 246.

39. Emil L. Fackenheim, *The Jewish Return Into History* (New York: Schocken Books, 1978), 79.

40. Langdon Gilkey, *Message and Existence: An Introduction to Christian Theology* (New York: Seabury, 1980), 163, 164, 165, 171, 173, 174–176, and *passim*.

41. Steven T. Katz, *Post-Holocaust Dialogues* (New York: New York University Press, 1983), 149.

42. Jean Daniélou, *Dialogue with Israel* (Baltimore: Helicon, 1966), 99.

43. Jürgen Moltmann, *The Trinity and the Kingdom: The Doctrine of God*, trans. Margaret Kohl (San Francisco: Harper & Row, 1981), 122–124.

44. For example, Jürgen Moltmann, "Messianic Hope in Christianity," in Küng and Kasper, eds., *Christians and Jews*, 65–66.

45. Pinchas Lapide, *The Resurrection of Jesus: A Jewish Perspective*, trans. Wilhelm C. Linss (Minneapolis: Augsburg, 1983); Carl E. Braaten, Introduction to Lapide, 23ff.

46. Robert A. Everett, conversations, Jan. 16–17, 1985.

47. J. (Coos) Schoneveld, "The Jewish 'No' to Jesus and the Christian 'Yes' to Jews," *Quarterly Review* 4 (1984): 60, 63; slightly emended.

48. John T. Pawlikowski, *What Are They Saying About Christian-Jewish Relations?*, 107.

49. Rose G. Lewis, "James Parkes: Christianity without Anti-Semitism," *MID* 28 (1982): 43.

50. Paul Tillich, "You Are Accepted," *The Shaking of the Foundations* (New York: Scribner, 1948), 153–163.

51. Martin A. Cohen, "The Mission of Israel after Auschwitz," in Helga Croner and Leon Klenicki, eds., *Issues in the Jewish-Christian Dialogue*, 162.

52. Irving Greenberg, "Polarity and Perfection," *FF* 6 (1979): 14.

53. Fackenheim, *To Mend the World*, 39.

54. See Eugene B. Borowitz, *Choices in Modern Jewish Thought: A Partisan Guide* (New York: Behrman, 1983), 214–215.

55. Cf. Fackenheim: "We cannot, on the grounds that all men are sinners,

dissolve or weaken the distinction between those who *might* have done it [viz., carried out the *Endlösung*] and those who *did* it. This latter is especially tempting to Christians" (Fackenheim, *To Mend the World*, 235).

6. Irons in the Public Fire

1. Robert T. Handy, *A Christian America* (New York: Oxford University Press, 1971), 215.

2. Robert Gordis, "The Revival of Religion and the Decay of Ethics," *CC* 101 (1984): 1122–1126.

3. Consult *The Documents of Vatican II*, ed. Walter M. Abbott (New York: Guild-America-Association, 1966), "Declaration on Religious Freedom," 675–696; "Declaration on the Apostolate of the Laity," 489–521; "Decree on the Bishops' Pastoral Office in the Church," 396–429; also, on religious freedom, John T. Pawlikowski, "Method in Catholic Social Ethics: Some Observations in Light of the Jewish Tradition," in Eugene J. Fisher and Daniel F. Polish, eds., *The Formation of Social Policy in the Catholic and Jewish Traditions*, 173ff.

4. Rosemary Ruether, "Is a New Christian Consensus Possible?" *Journal of Ecumenical Studies* 17 (1980): 64, 65.

5. Yechiel Eckstein, *What Christians Should Know About Jews and Judaism*, 309.

6. Tom F. Driver, "Hating Jews for Jesus' Sake," *Christianity and Crisis* 40 (1980): 325, 333, 335.

7. Larry Cohler, "Fundamentalist 'talent bank' aided by Merit Systems chief," *Jewish World*, Jan. 25–31, 1985; William Bole, "Looking Toward 1988," *PT* 12 (1985): 25–26; "Church-State Separation is Still Sacred," *Business Week*, Sept. 24, 1984, 24; Arthur E. Gay, Jr., "Remarks on Church-State Relations," paper at Anti-Defamation League–Lilly Foundation Institute on Jewish-Christian Relations, Indiana University, Dec. 10–13, 1984; "Bishop Criticizes Mixing of Church and State," *NYT*, Nov. 4, 1984; David Earle Anderson, "Myths and Simplifications," *PT* 12 (1985): 39; Sol Roth, "Methodology and Social Policy: A Jewish Perspective," in Fisher and Polish, eds., *Formation of Social Policy*, 153; Robert N. Bellah, "Toward Clarity in the Midst of Conflict," *Christianity and Crisis* 44 (1984): 392.

8. Handy, *Christian America*, 214.

9. Stuart E. Rosenberg, *The New Jewish Identity in America*, 195–196.

10. Henry Steel Commager, "Public Morality, Not Religion," *NYT*, Sept. 16, 1984.

11. Gay, "Remarks on Church-State Relations."

12. See Rosenberg, *New Jewish Identity in America*, chap. 12.

13. Handy, *Christian America*, 214.

14. Consult Robert C. Liebman and Robert Wuthnow, *The New Christian Right: Mobilization and Legitimation* (New York: Aldine, 1983).

15. Tim LaHaye, as cited in Bole, "Looking Toward 1988," 27; Larry Cohler, "The Jewish Link," *PT* 12 (1985): 36.

16. Alice and Roy Eckardt, "The Achievements and Trials of Interfaith," *Judaism* 27 (1978): 318.

17. Marc H. Tanenbaum, "The Concept of the Human Being in Jewish Thought: Some Ethical Implications," in Tanenbaum, Marvin R. Wilson, and A. James Rudin, eds., *Evangelicals and Jews in an Age of Pluralism*, 52.

18. Alice L. Eckardt, "Power and Powerlessness: The Jewish Experience," in Israel W. Charny, ed., *Toward the Understanding and Prevention of Genocide* (Boulder/London: Westview, 1984), 187.

19. A senior White House official, as cited in "On Terrorism," *American Foreign Policy Newsletter*, National Committee on American Foreign Policy, 6 (1984): 15.

20. "On Terrorism."

21. Eliezer Berkovits, *With God in Hell: Judaism in the Ghettos and Death-camps* (New York: Sanhedrin, 1979), 155, 156.

22. Milton Steinberg, *Basic Judaism* (New York: Harcourt, Brace, 1947), 76.

23. Robert L. Brashear, "Corner-Stone, Stumbling-Stone: Christian Problems in Viewing Israel," *Union Seminary Quarterly Review* 38 (1983): 219.

24. See, in general, the serial *Quaker Life;* also, Rael Jean Isaac, "The Seduction of the Quakers: From Friendly Persuasion to P.L.O. Support," *MID* 25 (1979): 23–29; H. David Kirk, *The Friendly Perversion, Quakers as Reconcilers: Good People and Dirty Work* (New York: Americans for a Safe Israel, 1979); Robert J. Loewenberg, "The Violent Quakers," *MID* 28 (1982): 15–18; Marvin Mauer, "Quakers in Politics: Israel, P.L.O., and Social Revolution," *MID* 23 (1977): 36–44; "Quakers and Communists: Vietnam and Israel," *MID* 25 (1979): 30–35.

25. Asia A. Bennett, Executive Secretary, American Friends Service Committee, letter to *Jerusalem Post International Edition*, week ending Oct. 6, 1984, 23.

26. Loewenberg, "Violent Quakers," 15–17.

27. Eliezer Berkovits, "Facing the Truth," *Judaism* 27 (1978): 326.

28. "Nuns Say They Got a Vatican Threat," *NYT*, Dec. 15, 1984; "Vatican Threat on Abortion Ad Went to Signers," *NYT*, Dec. 19, 1984; "Nuns, Expressing Dismay, Ponder Vatican Threat," *NYT*, Dec. 20, 1984; "Most Women Religious Resist Vatican's Retraction Demand," *National Catholic Reporter*, Dec. 28, 1984; "Nuns' Superiors Ask Moderation By the Vatican," *NYT*, Jan. 11, 1985; "Nuns Say Vatican Threat Imperils Catholics' Rights to Speak Freely," *NYT*, Jan. 27, 1985.

29. *Documents of Vatican II*, "Declaration on Religious Freedom."

30. Dennis Crowley, letter in *NYT*, Jan. 2, 1985.

31. David M. Feldman, *Jewish Views on Abortion*, as cited in *CC* 101 (1984): 1032; Feldman, *Marital Relations, Birth Control, and Abortion in Jewish Law* (New York: Schocken, 1978), part three, "Abortion."

32. "Nuns accuse bishops of 'sexism' on abortion," *Bethlehem (Pa.) Globe-Times*, Oct. 11, 1984.

33. "Statement on the Current Abortion Debate," National Coalition of American Nuns, Oct. 8, 1984; Madonna Kolbenschlag, "Abortion and Moral Consensus: Beyond Solomon's Choice," *CC* 102 (1985): 183.

7. Enter the Women's Movement

1. Deborah McCauley and Annette Daum, "Jewish-Christian-Feminist Dialogue: A Wholistic Vision," *Union Seminary Quarterly Review* 38 (1983): 147–190.

2. "Statement on the Current Abortion Debate," National Coalition of American Nuns, Oct. 8, 1984.

3. Madonna Kolbenschlag, "Abortion and Moral Consensus: Beyond Solomon's Choice," *CC* 102 (1985): 179, 180.

4. *St. Louis Review* (weekly newspaper of the Catholic Archdiocese of St. Louis), Oct. 26, 1984.

5. Editorial, "Paul and the Bishops on Dignity and Community," *Christianity and Crisis* 44 (1985): 507.

6. "Women of the Cloth: How They're Faring," *U.S. News & World Report*, Dec. 3, 1984, 76–77; "Women as Parish Clergy," *CC* 102 (1985): 72. The latter report is criticized as misleading by Jane Searjeant Watt and Diana J. Vezmar, letter to *CC* 102 (1985): 254.

7. Ann Patrick Ware, "Some Theses for Discussion," Seminar on Images of Women in Christian and Jewish Traditions, 8th National Workshop on Christian-Jewish Relations, St. Louis, Oct. 29–Nov. 1, 1984.

8. Ibid.

9. Letty Cottin Pogrebin, "Women as the Litmus Test" (part of a symposium), PT 12 (1985): 46–47.

10. Adler's reference to slavery could seem anachronistic in light of that institution's abandonment long ago. Her response, I should imagine, would be to point out that the passage of time has not freed women. Hence, the comparative allusion to slavery is as fitting as ever. Rachel Adler, "The Jew Who Wasn't There: Halacha and the Jewish Woman," in Menachem Marc Kellner, ed., *Contemporary Jewish Ethics*, 348–349.

11. Ware, "Some Theses for Discussion."

12. See, for example, Rochelle Furstenberg, "Points of Conflict," *Jerusalem Post International Edition*, week ending Oct. 6, 1984, 19.

13. McCauley and Daum, "Jewish-Christian-Feminist Dialogue," 164.

14. Ibid., 174, 151, 176, 182.

15. Ibid., 178–179.

16. See Leonard Swidler, *Biblical Affirmations of Woman* (Philadelphia: Westminster, 1979), 353.

17. McCauley and Daum, "Jewish-Christian-Feminist Dialogue," 181.

18. Annette Daum, "A Jewish Feminist View," *Theology Today* 41 (1984): 300.

19. McCauley and Daum, "Jewish-Christian-Feminist Dialogue," 175.

20. This typology is adapted from George E. Rupp, "Commitment in a Pluralistic World," in Leroy S. Rouner, ed., *Religious Pluralism,* 219.

21. See Irving Greenberg, "The Religious Argument Over Feminism," *Perspectives,* National Jewish Resource Center, January 1985, 2.

22. Consult Carol Gilligan, *A Different Voice: Psychological Theory and Women's Development* (Cambridge: Harvard University Press, 1982).

23. J. Coert Rylaarsdam, "Judaism: The Christian Problem," *FF* 11 (1984): 5.

24. Dorothee Sölle, "Christianity and the Jewish Request for Signs: A Reflection on I Corinthians 1:22," *FF* 11 (1984): 20.

25. Ibid.
26. Ibid.

8. Along the Road of Good Intentions

1. Joseph E. Monti, *Who Do You Say That I Am? The Christian Understanding of Christ and Antisemitism* (New York: Paulist, 1984). The quoted passage is from pp. 77–78.

2. H. Richard Niebuhr, *The Meaning of Revelation* (New York: Macmillan, 1941), 44–54.

3. Ronald Goetz, "A Lived Resurrection," *CC* 100 (1983): 263–264.

4. See Karl Rahner, *Foundations of Christian Faith: An Introduction to the Idea of Christianity*, trans. William V. Dych (New York: Seabury, 1978), chap. 6; John Hick, "Religious Pluralism and Absolute Claims," in Rouner, ed., *Religious Pluralism*, 201–205.

5. Pope John Paul II, as cited by Eugene J. Fisher, in review of Lawrence McCoombe and Annette Daum, eds., *Jews and Christians, Union Seminary Quarterly Review* 38 (1983): 24.

6. Paul M. van Buren, *A Christian Theology of the People Israel* (New York: Seabury, 1983); Franz Mussner, *Tractate On the Jews: The Significance of Judaism for Christian Faith*, trans. Leonard Swidler (Philadelphia: Fortress, 1984); Clemens Thoma, *A Christian Theology of Judaism*, trans. Helga Croner (New York: Paulist, 1980).

7. A. Roy Eckardt, "Anti-Semitism is the Heart," *Theology Today* 41 (1984): 302.

8. John T. Pawlikowski, *Christ in the Light of the Christian-Jewish Dialogue*, 109, 117–118.

9. David S. Shapiro, "The Doctrine of the Image of God and Imitatio Dei," in Menachem Marc Kellner, ed., *Contemporary Jewish Ethics*, 128.

9. Somewhere Another Road

1. Jacob Katz, *From Prejudice to Destruction: Anti-Semitism, 1700–1933* (Cambridge: Harvard University Press, 1980), 326.

2. Martin A. Cohen, "The Mission of Israel after Auschwitz," in Helga Croner and Leon Klenicki, eds., *Issues in the Jewish-Christian Dialogue*, 169.

3. Irving Greenberg, "Cloud of Smoke, Pillar of Fire: Judaism, Christianity, and Modernity after the Holocaust," in Eva Fleischner, ed., *Auschwitz*, 23.

4. A. Roy Eckardt, "Recent Literature on Christian-Jewish Relations," *Journal of the American Academy of Religion* 49 (1981): 106.

5. David Tracy, "Historicism, Historicity, and Holocaust," unpublished paper at Scholars' Conference on "Thinking About the Holocaust," Indiana University, Bloomington, Nov. 3–5, 1980.

6. Donald A. Hagner, *The Jewish Reclamation of Jesus* (Grand Rapids: Academie Books–Zondervan, 1984), 298.

7. Samuel Sandmel, *We Jews and Jesus* (New York: Oxford University Press, 1965), 151.

8. Rosemary Radford Ruether, *Disputed Questions: On Being a Christian* (Nashville: Abingdon, 1982), 47.

9. Paul Tillich, *The Courage to Be* (New Haven: Yale University Press, 1952).

10. See Irving Greenberg, "Developing the Image of God or, Judaism: 24 Hours a Day, 7 Days a Week," *Perspectives*, National Jewish Resource Center, February 1985, 5–6.

11. John Hick, *The Center of Christianity* (San Francisco: Harper & Row, 1978).

12. For a beginning effort toward a theocentric, non-exclusivist, non-imperialist Christology, consult Paul F. Knitter, *No Other Name? A Critical Survey of Christian Attitudes Toward the World Religions*, 175; see especially 182–185, 197–200. Knitter writes: "Christocentrism without theocentrism easily becomes an idolatry that violates not only Christian revelation but the revelation found in other faiths." However, Knitter's work is subject to the criticism respecting the problem of truth that is made of Joseph E. Monti (and of H. Richard Niebuhr) in chapter eight above. Knitter's affirmations upon the Resurrection are especially open to the difficulties considered at various places in the present essay.

BIBLIOGRAPHY

This listing (primarily of books) is selective and abbreviated, and it is limited, with some exceptions, to recent publications. Further sources of relevance are found in the references cited in the present study.

Bauer, Yehuda, *The Jewish Emergence from Powerlessness* (Toronto: University of Toronto Press, 1979).

Berkovits, Eliezer, *Not in Heaven: The Nature and Function of Halakha* (New York: Ktav, 1983).

Boadt, Lawrence, Helga Croner, and Leon Klenicki, eds., *Biblical Studies: Meeting Ground of Jews and Christians* (Ramsey, N.J.: Paulist, 1981).

Borowitz, Eugene B., *Contemporary Christologies: A Jewish Response* (New York: Paulist, 1980).

Brown, Robert McAfee, *Elie Wiesel: Messenger to All Humanity* (Notre Dame: University of Notre Dame Press, 1983).

Cohen, Arthur A., *The Tremendum: A Theological Interpretation of the Holocaust* (New York: Crossroad, 1981).

Cohen, Martin A., and Helga Croner, eds., *Christian Mission/Jewish Mission* (Ramsey, N.J.: Paulist, 1982).

Croner, Helga, ed., *More Stepping Stones to Jewish-Christian Relations: An Unabridged Collection of Christian Documents 1975–1983* (Ramsey, N.J.: Paulist, 1985).

———, compiler. *Stepping Stones to Further Jewish-Christian Relations* (London/New York: Stimulus Books, 1977).

Croner, Helga, and Leon Klenicki, eds., *Issues in the Jewish-Christian Dialogue: Jewish Perspectives on Covenant, Mission and Witness* (New York: Paulist, 1979).

Davies, Alan T., ed., *Anti-Semitism and the Foundations of Christianity* (New York: Paulist, 1979).

Davies, W. D., *The Territorial Dimension of Judaism* (Berkeley: University of California Press, 1982).

Douglas, Mary, and Steven Tipton, eds., *Religion and America: Spiritual Life in a Secular Age* (Boston: Beacon, 1983).

Driver, Tom F., *Christ in a Changing World: Toward an Ethical Christology* (New York: Crossroad, 1981).

Eckardt, A. Roy, *Elder and Younger Brothers: The Encounter of Jews and Christians* (New York: Schocken Books, 1973).

———. "Recent Literature on Christian-Jewish Relations," *Journal of the American Academy of Religion* 49 (1981): 99–111.

Eckardt, A. Roy, and Alice L. Eckardt, *Long Night's Journey Into Day: Life and Faith After the Holocaust*, rev. ed. (New York: Holocaust Library, 1986).

Eckstein, Yechiel, *What Christians Should Know about Jews and Judaism* (Waco: Word Books, 1984).

Eisen, Arnold M., *The Chosen People in America* (Bloomington: Indiana University Press, 1983).

Everett, Robert A., *James Parkes: Historian and Theologian of Jewish-Christian Relations* (Ann Arbor: University Microfilms International, 1983).

Fackenheim, Emil L., *To Mend the World: Foundations of Future Jewish Thought* (New York: Schocken Books, 1982).

Fiorenza, Elisabeth Schüssler, and Mary Collins, eds., *Women—Invisible in Church Theology*, Concilium series 182 (Edinburgh: T. & T. Clark, 1985).

Fiorenza, Elisabeth Schüssler, and David Tracy, eds., *The Holocaust as Interruption*, Concilium series 175 (Edinburgh: T. & T. Clark, 1984).

Flannery, Edward H., *The Anguish of the Jews*, rev. ed. (Ramsey, N.J.: Paulist, 1985).

Fleischner, Eva, ed., *Auschwitz: Beginning of a New Era? Reflections on the Holocaust* (New York: Ktav, 1977).

Gager, John G., *The Origins of Anti-Semitism: Attitudes Toward Judaism in Pagan and Christian Antiquity* (New York: Oxford University Press, 1983).

Glazer, Nathan, *American Judaism*, 2nd rev. ed. (Chicago: University of Chicago Press, 1972).

Goldberg, Michael, *Jews and Christians, Getting Our Stories Straight: The Exodus and the Passion-Resurrection* (Nashville: Abingdon, 1985).

Greenberg, Blu, *On Women and Judaism: A View from Tradition* (Philadelphia: Jewish Publication Society of America, 1981).

Greenberg, Irving, *The Third Great Cycle in Jewish History* (New York: National Jewish Resource Center, 1981).

———. *Voluntary Covenant* (New York: National Jewish Resource Center, 1982).

Greenstein, Howard R., *Judaism—An Eternal Covenant* (Philadelphia: Fortress, 1983).

Grose, Peter, *Israel in the Mind of America* (New York: Knopf, 1983).

Gustafson, James M., *Ethics from a Theocentric Perspective*, 2 vols. (Chicago: University of Chicago Press, 1981, 1984).

Handy, Robert T., *History of the Churches in the United States and Canada* (New York: Oxford University Press, 1977).

Hennesey, James, *American Catholics: A History of the Roman Catholic Community in the United States* (New York: Oxford University Press, 1981).

Heschel, Susannah, ed., *On Being A Jewish Feminist: A Reader* (New York: Schocken Books, 1983).

Heyward, Isabel Carter, *The Redemption of God: A Theology of Mutual Relation* (Washington: University Press of America, 1982).

Jacob, Walter, *Christianity Through Jewish Eyes: The Quest for Common Ground* (Cincinnati: Hebrew Union College Press, 1974).

Jansen, John Frederick, *The Resurrection of Jesus Christ in New Testament Theology* (Philadelphia: Westminster, 1980).

Jocz, Jacob, *The Jewish People and Jesus Christ After Auschwitz* (Grand Rapids: Baker, 1981).

Johnson, Paul, *A History of Christianity* (London: Weidenfeld and Nicolson, 1976).

Kellner, Menachem Marc, ed., *Contemporary Jewish Ethics* (New York: Sanhedrin, 1978).

Klausner, Joseph, *The Messianic Idea in Israel,* trans. W. F. Stinespring (New York: Macmillan, 1955).

Knitter, Paul F., *No Other Name? A Critical Survey of Christian Attitudes toward the World Religions* (Maryknoll, N.Y.: Orbis Books, 1985).

Lapide, Pinchas, *Israelis, Jews, and Jesus,* trans. Peter Heinegg (Garden City: Doubleday, 1979).

Lapide, Pinchas, and Jürgen Moltmann, *Jewish Monotheism and Christian Trinitarian Doctrine* (Philadelphia: Fortress, 1980).

Littell, Franklin H., *The Crucifixion of the Jews: The Failure of Christians to Understand the Jewish Experience* (New York: Harper & Row, 1975).

McGarry, Michael B., *Christology After Auschwitz* (New York: Paulist, 1977).

Macquarrie, John, *Principles of Christian Theology,* 2nd ed. (New York: Scribner, 1977).

Marty, Martin E., *Pilgrims in Their Own Land: 500 Years of Religion in America* (Boston: Little, Brown, 1984).

Parkes, James, *The Foundations of Judaism and Christianity* (London: Vallentine, Mitchell, 1960).

―――. *Whose Land? A History of the Peoples of Palestine* (New York: Taplinger, 1971).

Pawlikowski, John T., *Christ in the Light of the Christian-Jewish Dialogue* (New York: Paulist, 1982).

―――. *What Are They Saying About Christian-Jewish Relations?* (New York: Paulist, 1980).

Peck, Abraham J., ed., *Jews and Christians After the Holocaust* (Philadelphia: Fortress, 1982).

Perlmutter, Nathan, and Ruth Ann Perlmutter, *The Real Anti-Semitism in America* (New York: Arbor House, 1982).

Religious Freedom in America: Essays in Historical Interpretation, ed. Gillian Lindt and James Waller, special issue of *Union Seminary Quarterly Review* 38 (1984).

Rosenberg, Stuart E., *The New Jewish Identity in America* (New York: Hippocrene Books, 1984).

Rouner, Leroy S., ed., *Religious Pluralism* (Notre Dame: University of Notre Dame Press, 1984).

Rousseau, Richard W., ed., *Christianity and Judaism: The Deepening Dialogue* (Montrose, Pa.: Ridge Row Press, 1983).

Rudin, A. James, *Israel for Christians* (Philadelphia: Fortress, 1983).

Ruether, Rosemary Radford, *Faith and Fratricide: The Theological Roots of Anti-Semitism* (New York: Seabury, 1974).

―――. *Sexism and God-Talk: Toward a Feminist Theology* (Boston: Beacon, 1983).

Sanders, E. P., *Jesus and Judaism* (Philadelphia: Fortress, 1985).

―――. *Paul, the Law, and the Jewish People* (Philadelphia: Fortress, 1983).

Sandmel, Samuel, *Anti-Semitism in the New Testament?* (Philadelphia: Fortress, 1978).

Seltzer, Robert M., *Jewish People, Jewish Thought: The Jewish Experience in History* (New York: Macmillan, 1980).

Soloveitchik, Joseph B., *Halakhic Man* (Philadelphia: Jewish Publication Society, 1984).

Talmage, Frank Ephraim, ed., *Disputation and Dialogue: Readings in the Jewish-Christian Encounter* (New York: Ktav, 1975).

Tanenbaum, Marc H., A. James Rudin, and Marvin Wilson, eds., *Evangelicals and Jews in an Age of Pluralism* (Grand Rapids: Baker, 1984).

Vermes, Geza, *Jesus and the World of Judaism* (Philadelphia: Fortress, 1984).

Volkman, Ernest, *A Legacy of Hate: Anti-Semitism in America* (New York: Franklin Watts, 1982).

Weiss-Rosmarin, Trude, ed., *Jewish Expressions on Jesus: An Anthology* (New York: Ktav, 1977).

Williamson, Clark M., *Has God Rejected His People?: Anti-Judaism in the Christian Church* (Nashville: Abingdon, 1982).

Journals
Christian Jewish Relations (London).
Face to Face (New York).
Holocaust and Genocide Studies (Oxford).
Immanuel (Jerusalem).
Journal of Ecumenical Studies (Philadelphia).
Sidic (Rome).

INDEX

A. ROY ECKARDT is emeritus professor of religion studies at Lehigh University; former editor-in-chief of the *Journal of the American Academy of Religion;* currently a visiting scholar at the Oxford Centre for Hebrew Studies; and author of many books, including *Long Night's Journey into Day* and *Elder and Younger Brothers*.